The One-Minute Aquinas

Other books by Kevin Vost
from Sophia Institute Press:

Memorize the Faith!
Unearthing Your Ten Talents
Fit for Eternal Life!

KEVIN VOST

The One-Minute
AQUINAS

THE DOCTOR'S QUICK ANSWERS
TO FUNDAMENTAL QUESTIONS

SOPHIA INSTITUTE PRESS
Manchester, New Hampshire

Except where otherwise noted, biblical references in this book are taken from the Douay-Rheims edition of the Old and New Testaments. References followed by "RSV" are taken from the Revised Standard Version of the Bible, copyright 1952 (2nd edition, 1971) by the Division of Christian Education of the National Council of the Churches of Christ in the United States of America. Used by permission. All rights reserved.

Sophia Institute Press
Box 5284, Manchester, NH 03108
1-800-888-9344

www.SophiaInstitute.com

Sophia Institute Press® is a registered trademark of Sophia Institute.

Library of Congress Cataloging-in-Publication Data
Vost, Kevin.
    The one-minute Aquinas : the doctor's quick answers to fundamental questions, St. Thomas Aquinas / Kevin Vost.
        pages cm
    Includes bibliographical references.
    ISBN 978-1-622821-58-7 (pbk. : alk. paper) 1. Thomas, Aquinas, Saint, 1225?-1274. Summa theologica. I. Title.
    BX1749.T6V67 2014
    230'.2—dc23

                                                                2013040127

First printing

To Sisters Matthew Marie Cummings, Elizabeth
Anne Allen, and Mary Anne Zuberbueler, O.P.,
the Dominican Sisters of St. Cecilia,
and the faculty, staff, and students
of Aquinas College in Nashville, Tennessee,
for the glorious way that you share
the fruits of your contemplation.

Because he had the utmost reverence for the Doctors of antiquity, he seems to have inherited in a way the intellect of all.

— Pope Leo XIII, *Aeterni Patris*

He could have discovered philosophy anew, if it had been destroyed by fire. He could have restored it in a better way: his knowledge entitled him to fame, greater even than that of the ancients.

— Henry of Wurzberg, poet

St. Thomas cast his net upon the universe and carried off all things, transformed into the life of the mind, towards the beatific vision.

— Jacques Maritain, *St. Thomas Aquinas*

Contents

Part II

God

Part III

Who Is Christ?

Preface

The world's smartest man?

Who is the world's smartest man? This is not the world's easiest question to answer. It's not like trying to find the world's *strongest* man, where you can gather enormous barbells, boulders, trucks, and the like to see who can lift, heave, and pull them the best. And besides, I don't just mean the smartest man alive *today*, but the smartest person of *all time*.

How about Albert Einstein? It's not every day that some guy figures out that $E = mc^2$ (whatever exactly that means). Many say Einstein did Sir Isaac Newton (the father of the three Laws of Motion) one better when it came to grasping the mysteries of the physical universe.

Then there's Aristotle, "the Father of Logic." When modern social scientist Charles Murray wrote his book *Human Accomplishment*, comparing the most influential thinkers in science, philosophy, literature, and art, this fellow from ancient Greece was the all-time, all-around MVP, and easily number one in philosophy. In addition, Murray ranks Aristotle second only to Charles Darwin in the field of biology. Indeed, when Darwin read Aristotle for the first time, he wrote that, although Linnaeus and Cuvier had been his "gods," he found they were "mere schoolboys to old Aristotle."

There's another candidate all lovers of science should know. He was one of the most prolific writers of all time, the most famous German professor of his day—a veritable one-man walking encyclopedia who wrote on every topic from A (as in anatomy, anthropology, and astronomy) to Z (zoology). He was such a towering mind that he was called *Magnus* ("the Great") while he still lived. He is the patron saint of scientists and scholars—St. Albert the Great (1193–1280). But Albert the Great had a hero he considered much greater than himself. That hero was so brilliant that when Albert read the man's crowning masterpiece, he ceased writing himself, explaining that his hero's work could not be equaled or surpassed. Who was the hero? St. Albert's own former student, St. Thomas Aquinas (1225–1274). When Thomas died at the age of forty-nine, St. Albert bemoaned the loss of "the flower and glory of the world."

It's St. Thomas Aquinas who I (and many others) believe is the smartest human being God ever graced to walk upon the earth.

Who says St. Thomas is smart?

Not that St. Thomas himself claimed to be a genius. In the first book of his masterful *Summa Contra Gentiles*, he apologized to his readers that in attempting the work, he might be exceeding his "limited powers," but he embarked nonetheless with confidence "in the name of divine Mercy."

But since St. Thomas's passing on March 7, 1274, more than seven hundred years of popes, scholars, and saints have agreed that his wisdom and powers, rather than being "limited," were so extraordinary that he is called the Angelic Doctor.

Atheistic philosophers, including the Objectivist followers of Ayn Rand, acknowledge St. Thomas's towering achievements in the field of reason and in reviving and disseminating the works of Aristotle. Charles Murray, an agnostic, lists St. Thomas among the "giants" of western philosophy, ranking him the sixth most influential of all time—above Socrates and St. Augustine. Note that philosophy was not Thomas's specialty, but merely a tool—a "handmaiden" to theology, the highest of all branches of learning.

Thomas makes this crystal clear: "To use the words of [St.] Hilary: 'I am aware that I owe this to God as the chief duty of my life: that my every word and sense may speak of Him.'"[1]

When groups of modern psychologists have been polled on the most defining characteristic of superior human intelligence, time and again the winner is *the capacity for abstract reasoning.* That's the ability to see the concrete things and events in the world and to grasp their underlying causes and principles; and also to go the other way: to grasp the fundamental, universal principles of reality and apply them to particular things and events.

That gift was St. Thomas's strong suit and was crucial to his massive contribution to civilization—which was to teach us how to reason in God's world and find our way to real wisdom. As Thomas himself put it: "Experience shows that some understand more profoundly than do others; as one who carries a conclusion to its first principles and ultimate causes understands it better than one who reduces it to its proximate causes."[2] As we will see in Part I of this book, St. Thomas even explains for us just how abstract reasoning works. He devoted the full power of his intellect, throughout his whole life, to the highest, most

[1] *Summa Contra Gentiles,* I, 2, 2.
[2] *Summa Theologica,* I, Q. 85, art. 7, p. 439.

important, and fundamental cause. As he will tell us in Part II of this book: "And this we call God."

The people's genius

But note well, Thomas was anything but an "egghead" or a modern academic with his head in the clouds, writing only for other professors and university students. As a spiritual son of St. Dominic and member of his Order of Friars Preachers, Thomas used also his great intellectual gifts to explain Christ's gospel message to the minds and hearts of ordinary lay folk. As a young man, after receiving Holy Orders in Cologne, his sermons in the German vernacular (rather than in Latin) drew enormous crowds. In the last year of his life, he preached a series of sermons in the Neapolitan dialect at the church of San Domenico in Naples that, according to early biographers, drew "almost the whole population of Naples," and indeed, "he was heard by the people with such reverence that it was as if his preaching came forth from God."[3] St. Thomas, then, was a man of thought, a man of God, and a man of the common people.

[3] Ralph McInerny citing John Coppa of Naples and William of Tocco in *The Aquinas Catechism: A Simple Explanation of the Catholic Faith by the Church's Greatest Theologian* (Manchester, NH: Sophia Institute Press, 2000), xi. (Indeed, if you'd care to sample these wonderful sermons, *The Aquinas Catechism* is based on summaries of those sermons by St. Thomas's friend, Reginald of Piperno. McInerny wrote in the foreword that Thomas's sermons on the Apostles' Creed could be called "a *Summa* for the simple!" (p. xii). And just how important did Thomas himself consider this popular preaching? He said the following near the start of his very first sermon on the value of faith: "Before the coming of Christ none of the philosophers was able, however great his effort, to know as much about

Preface

There's no point in being smart unless you're wise. As "old Aristotle" said: "It is better to know a little about sublime things than a lot about mean things." In other words, since none of us can know everything, the wise man will focus his attention on the things that matter the most, and that is something St. Thomas did like few who lived before him or since.

God or about the means necessary for obtaining eternal life, as any old woman knows by faith since Christ came down upon earth" (p. 6).

Acknowledgments

A thousand thanks and more to Charlie McKinney, Carolyn McKinney, Duncan Maxwell Anderson, Sheila Perry, Nora Malone, and all the staff of Sophia Institute Press, for rendering the potentiality of *The One-Minute Aquinas* into full actuality within the bounds of one year.

The Questions That Matter Most

What matters most to you? Chances are I don't know you, but because you are reading this book, I know you are a human person created in the image and likeness of God (Gen. 1:26). Of all of the species of creatures on earth, I am confident that no other, not even your pet chimpanzee or dolphin, is reading this to you. I know that you have an intellect and a will.

I also know what matters most to you. The most important thing that you seek is *happiness*.[4] If you are a Christian, then, you also realize that while some happiness can come upon earth, our ultimate happiness comes in an eternal life with God, the origin and end of all that is good and which makes us happy. I'm willing to wager as well that you'd very much like for your family and friends to share in this bliss with you. And if you've taken the message of God's Son to heart, you desire the same for your neighbor—that is, for all of mankind.

Well then, it stands to reason that nothing matters more than our relationship with God, and no subject could be more

---

[4] In case you'd beg to differ, I'll provide St. Thomas's own arguments right off the bat in chapter 1.

important than learning just how to improve it—how to, in the words of the prayer of St. Richard of Chichester, "know Thee more clearly, love Thee more dearly, follow Thee more nearly."[5] This is why the writings of St. Thomas are so important to us: He so fully submitted his unusual human powers to the stirrings of the Holy Spirit. There is no greater guide on earth, to knowing, loving, and following God while we are *viators* ("travelers") here, on our way to seeing God in the eternal beatific vision.

St. Thomas provides sublimely profound answers to the questions that matter the most—and yet he does not complicate things. He teaches us about our everyday lives:

What brings us happiness?
What does it mean to be a human being?
Why are we here?
In what ways are we higher than the animals and lower than the angels?
In what way are we made in the image and likeness of God?
How can we achieve our utmost potential?
How can we become brave, wise, and loving?
How can we become better friends?
Can we know if God really exists?
Can we understand God?
How can God be both One and Three?
Why did God become man?

[5] Cited in G.R. Bullock-Webster, *The Churchman's Prayer Manual* (London, 1913), 31; http://open.bu.edu/xmlui/bitstream/handle/2144/579/churchmansprayer00bulluoft.txt?sequence=1.

Introduction

What does Christ expect of members of his Church?
How can we obtain eternal bliss?

St. Thomas's *philosophia perennis*,[6] his timeless pearls of wisdom, are as relevant to us today as they were in the thirteenth century. Indeed, in some ways they are *more* relevant today, because we hear so many attempts to answer such all-important questions by relativistic, secular, and pseudoscientific systems of thought that are so influential now—and also are shallow, contradictory, and *wrong*!

As Blessed Pope John Paul II tells us in his encyclical *Fides et Ratio* ("Faith and Reason"), all men from all cultures and all times want to know, "Who am I? Where have I come from, and where am I going? Why is there evil? What is there after this life?"[7] There's no surer guide to those answers than St. Thomas Aquinas. John Paul says, "The Church has been justified in consistently proposing Saint Thomas as a master of thought and a model of the right way to do theology."[8]

Who was St. Thomas Aquinas?

Thomas Aquinas lived from approximately 1225 to March 7, 1274. The privileged seventh[9] child of an Italian lord and a relative of the imperial family, Thomas nonetheless sought the robe of a poor Dominican friar to live his life as a preacher and

---

6 Perennial or timeless philosophy.
7 *Fides et Ratio*, 1; http://www.vatican.va/holy_father/john_paul_ii/encyclicals/documents/hf_jp-ii_enc_15101998_fides-et-ratio_en.html.
8 Ibid, 43.
9 Thank God that Count Landulf of Aquino and Countess Theodora of Teano were so open to life!

teacher. He bore the gift of a marvelously powerful intellect and exercised it to the fullest. In early childhood, his most burning, repeated question to all was "What is God?" He spent his whole life seeking the answer. As a young man, he would study under the incomparably learned St. Albert the Great. He would spend the years of his mature adulthood as a teacher of theology, most notably at the University of Paris.

St. Thomas lived his life humbly and gently, absorbed in the contemplation of God and in sharing with others the fruits of his contemplation. He was perhaps the greatest integrator and synthesizer of truths in human history. He is the man who "baptized" Aristotle, the greatest of pagan philosophers, harnessing the truths Aristotle taught for the service of the Church. His knowledge of and reverence for the Church Fathers was so great that Pope Leo XIII declared in his encyclical *Aeterni Patris* that St. Thomas had "inherited the intellect of them all." But by far the greatest font of wisdom for Thomas was God's divine revelation provided in the Scriptures. The *Summa Theologica* absolutely bristles with scriptural citations and insights.

St. Thomas was canonized in 1323 and named a Doctor of the Church in 1567. He is known as the Angelic Doctor because of his detailed writings on the angels and because of his angelic demeanor.

What did St. Thomas's write? Some of his most notable works include:

Summa Contra Gentiles: A masterful work of more than 350,000 words explaining and defending the faith. Books 1 through 3 address theological issues accessible to human reason, such as God's existence and the fundamentals of human nature, while book 4 addresses issues of faith surpassing reason, such as the Trinity and the Incarnation.

Compendium of Theology:[10] A shorter, more accessible book addressing important theological issues for the layman. Written by a mature St. Thomas near the end of his life, it was dedicated to his friend Reginald of Piperno. Arranged in three parts under headings of Faith, Hope, and Charity, it is more than 350 pages long, but was never completed.

Commentaries on Aristotle: St. Thomas commented line-for-line on many of Aristotle's works. Two commentaries of great value to this writer have been on the *Nichomachean Ethics* (a wonderful treatise on virtue and friendship) and on Aristotle's *On the Soul* (a marvelous guide to human psychology). It's not every day you get one of the world's greatest minds commenting on another of them within the same book!

Biblical Commentaries: St. Thomas wrote penetrating commentaries on many books of the Bible. His *Catena Aurea* is an astounding "golden chain" of commentary from the Church Fathers (twenty-two Latin Fathers and fifty-three Greek Fathers) on every line of all four Gospels![11] His *Commentary on the Gospel of St. John* is especially rich and sublime.

---

[10] Available from Sophia Institute Press as *Aquinas's Shorter Summa.*

[11] The *Catena Aurea*, along with the *Summa Theologica*, was invaluable to me in writing *Unearthing Your Ten Talents*, on the parable of the talents in Matthew 25, and on St. Thomas's writings on ten fundamental virtues.

What about the *Summa Theologica*? (And how many frail, old librarians does it take to reshelve it?[12])

St. Thomas's magnum opus is his *Summa Theologica*. This unfinished work of the last seven years of his life is more than 1,500,000 words (3,000 pages) in length. It is a matchless synthesis of Scripture, philosophical wisdom, and Patristic insights of all the Latin and Greek Church Fathers before him. Three centuries after its composition, it sat alongside the Bible at the altar during the Council of Trent. It has been called a "Gothic cathedral of words."

The *Summa Theologica* contains thirty-eight treatises, each in itself a full-scale book by modern standards. The three major "parts" (summarized in this book, although not in the original order) are devoted to God, man, and Christ, respectively, and are interrelated in an overarching *exitus-reditus* (out from God, back to God) theme.

From God flows all creation, including man, who is made in his image and likeness. This is the stuff of Part I. Part II (subdivided into two parts of its own — I-II and II-II) focuses on man's return to God through an examination of moral living and virtue. Part III completes man's return to God via Christ and His Church. On the opposite page is a diagram of its fundamental structure.

The *Summa* is structured in a very formal way. Each of the three major parts, as we've noted, is divided into a series of questions (611 in all), and each question is divided into several

---

[12] Despite its great heft, it really doesn't require any, now that it's free online or as an e-book.

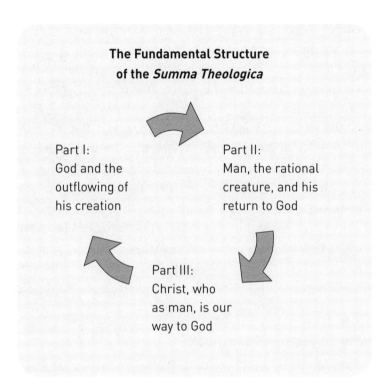

The Fundamental Structure
of the *Summa Theologica*

Part I:
God and the
outflowing of
his creation

Part II:
Man, the rational
creature, and his
return to God

Part III:
Christ, who
as man, is our
way to God

articles.[13] Each article, in turn, begins with the presentation of a few *objections*, including reference to the biblical or other sources from which they derive.

Thomas then states, "On the contrary" and provides a paragraph or so in which he typically includes a quotation in support of his conclusion. Next he states, "I answer that . . ." and

[13] Citations to the *Summa Theologica* in this book will note the part, the question, and the article, looking something like this: *ST*, I, Q. 25, art. 4. This would refer to the first part, question 25, article 4, which happens to be entitled "Whether God Can Make the Past Not to Have Been." (If you don't know St. Thomas's answer, please keep reading. You'll find out in chapter 24.)

proceeds to give his own, well-reasoned conclusions. Not finished yet, he replies to each one of the objections he presented at the start, typically revealing how the objection presented an incomplete or misconstrued interpretation of the scriptural, Patristic, or philosophical passage on which it was based.

Talk about rigorous reasoning and writing! But we have just a matter of minutes here. That's why I won't be able to provide all the wonderful give-and-take format of the original, along with all the great saint's citations. But thank God and St. Thomas we can go to the *Summa* itself for that. In this book, we will focus on the bottom lines that all those other lines point to. The bulk of our one-minute summaries will derive from St. Thomas's "I answer that . . ." conclusions, although we'll sometimes bring in his objections, citations, and replies to objections when they're helpful or entertaining.

Why do you need this book?

Sometimes, you want to get to the heart of things with one of the greatest minds in history, and you have only a minute (or two). St. Thomas could be called the Apostle of Common Sense. Yet his books are detailed and scholarly. One shudders to think of the intellectual prowess and academic background of the "beginners" to whom St. Thomas directed his *Summa Theologica*.[14] They were very learned seminary students. And although St. Thomas strove for brevity and died before the book's completion, it's more than 3,000 pages long, as we noted. The version I use is in five hefty volumes.

---

[14] *Summa Theologica*, prologue. Those theological "beginners" would have had previous training in philosophy to prepare them.

I assume the vast majority of Catholics have never read the *Summa Theologica*. Those who have even heard of it doubtless expect to find it full of profound theoretical reflections—which it is! But many would be surprised at what a practical and useful book it is too. Besides guiding us through common questions of faith, morals, the nature of God, and the many sides of human experience, Thomas gives us detailed, specific advice on how to perfect ourselves, with the help of God's grace—so that we may live more joyfully here on earth.

In *The One-Minute Aquinas*, we seek to provide the reader with a simple and swiftly readable summary of St. Thomas's greatest work in a book that is a fraction of the length of most *summaries* of the *Summa*—never mind the work itself. In these pages, you'll find small, digestible portions of life-giving wisdom and doctrine you can enjoy *one minute at a time*.

We will follow the *Summa Theologica*'s own unique order as we progress through this book, with one important modification. St. Thomas begins his *Summa* with quite heady stuff on the nature of God. But *The One-Minute Aquinas* is written for twenty-first-century lay readers. We thought it best to let readers start with questions covering the more familiar territory of human nature and happiness. Then, once your brain is warmed up and ready for action, we'll dive into Part II, on the existence, nature, and glories of God (Part I of the *Summa Theologica*). Both this book and the *Summa* conclude with Part III, on Christ and the sacraments.[15]

---

[15] Although it is not nearly as elegant as St. Thomas's *exitus-reditus* scheme, the weightlifter in me can't help thinking of Part I as our mental warm-up, Part II as the heart of our workout, and Part III as our refreshing cool-down.

What's here besides the *Summa*?

Most of the contents of this book will consist of summaries of St. Thomas's enlightening arguments and conclusions, although you will also find some commentary along the way, to help make things clear for modern readers. Further, we have felt free at times to add insights from St. Thomas's other writings besides the *Summa Theologica*, where relevant. There are also tables and graphics you're not going to find in the *Summa Theologica* itself. These are designed to help the modern reader grasp and remember St. Thomas's key ideas with a minimum of time and effort. By employing a fast-paced question-and-answer format — with most questions handled in one or two pages — we do what we can to turn timeless wisdom into easily digestible minutes.

What about those "Dumb Ox" boxes?

Thomas was barely out of his teens when he went to the University of Paris to study with St. Albert the Great. Judging from Thomas's massive frame and quiet demeanor, his fellow students assumed he was a not-very-bright country bumpkin. They called him the Dumb Ox of Sicily. (He wasn't from Sicily, but his mother was.) One day, one of those students offered to "help" the young ox with a difficult lesson. The normally taciturn Thomas proceeded to explain the passage to him with a depth of understanding that made the student's jaw drop.

St. Albert, their master, had been aware of Thomas's prodigious mental powers all along. He informed his students that the "bellowing" of the Dumb Ox would one day be heard around the world.

The "Dumb Ox" boxes you'll find periodically in this book are brief samples of St. Thomas's insights in answer to questions that surely have been nagging you for a lifetime — and to others that might not have occurred to you.

Got a minute?

Then what are we waiting for? Pope John XXII (1244–1334) said that starving Egyptians of old were told, "Go to Joseph," to receive corn to nourish their bodies. The Pope advised readers starving for the truth to "Go to Thomas, and ask him to give you from his ample store the food of substantial doctrine — wherewith to nourish your souls unto eternal life."

The One-Minute Aquinas

PART I

How Can We Be Happy — on Earth and in Heaven?

We shall consider first the last end of human life; and secondly, those things by means of which man may advance or stray from the path; for the end is the rule of whatever is ordained to the end. And since the last end of human life is happiness, we must consider (1) the last end in general; (2) happiness.

—ST, I-II, Q. 1. prologue

CHAPTER ONE

What Do We All Want? Happiness.

We have now to consider happiness; and (1) in what it consists; (2) what it is; (3) how we can obtain it.

—*ST*, I-II, Q. 2, prologue

Why do we act as we do? Unlike irrational animals driven by instinct, we have the power of reason to determine what seems good to us and the power of free will to choose what goods we will seek and how we will go about obtaining them. We are masters of our own actions. Those goods we seek are goals or ends, the things we hope to achieve by our actions. "Although the end be last in the order of execution, yet it is first in the order of the agent's intention. And it is in this way that it is a cause."[16]

Contrary to the tenets of twentieth-century radical-behaviorist psychology, St. Thomas recognized that we are not so much pawns who are *pushed* by the random events of our past as masters of our fates who are *pulled* by future goals of our own making.

[16] *ST*, I-II, Q. 1, art. 1.

In Aristotle's terms, an *end* acts as a *final cause*, a cause *for the sake of which* we undertake to do something. If you are surprised by a friend's actions and ask, "Why did you do that?" you assume that his behavior was not reflexive, like a sneeze, coerced at gunpoint, or in some other way involuntary. You're asking what he hoped to achieve — the *final cause* of his action, the *end* he had in mind. Aristotle and Aquinas argue that although each individual undeniably has his own personal likes and dislikes, we all act most of the time for the very *same* final, last end. So, what is that?

What is the one thing we all want?

According to St. Augustine, "all men agree in desiring the last end, which is happiness."[17] Why, then, do individual men (and women) act so very differently and achieve such differing degrees of happiness? St. Thomas notes that "to desire happiness is nothing else than to desire that one's will be satisfied. And this everyone desires." And yet, "all do not know Happiness; because they know not in what the general notion of happiness is found."[18] In other words, we all want to be happy, but not all of us know what really will make us happy. In determining what will bring us happiness, Thomas starts by enumerating some common false contenders — which are as popular and alluring today as they were in the thirteenth century.

Contrary to messages that "greed is good," "if it feels good, do it," "everybody wants to be a star [or an idol]," and "nice guys finish last," happiness does *not* consist in wealth, power, honor, fame and glory, goods of the body, pleasure, even goods

[17] *On the Trinity*, 13, 3. Cited in *ST*, I-II, Q. 1, art. 7.
[18] *ST*, I-II, Q. 6, art. 8.

of the soul—or for that manner, of *any* created good. These are only *means* to the *end* of happiness itself, and none of them ever completely satisfies. Sadly, they often lead to their possessor's and to others' destruction. The roster of rich and famous celebrities and sports superstars whose lives have ended in suicide or homicide bears witness to this fact. What, then, is true happiness?

Two kinds of happiness?

"The Philosopher [that is, Aristotle],[19] in placing man's happiness in this life (*Ethic.* i, 10), says it is imperfect, and after a long discussion concludes: *We call men happy, but only as men.* But God has promised us perfect happiness, when we shall be *as the angels . . . in heaven* (Matt. 22:30)."[20]

Thomas, informed by both natural reason and Christian revelation, acknowledges that we strive for a *twofold happiness*: 1) an *imperfect* happiness while here on earth and 2) a *perfect* happiness consisting of the beatific vision of the Uncreated Good (i.e., God) in heaven.

Augustine expressed this so beautifully, writing, "Our hearts are restless until they rest in you."[21] The "you," refers to God, the ultimate source of every good thing. Of course, we cannot obtain complete union with God until we reach heaven. In a most important sense, Thomas's end in writing the entire *Summa Theologica* is to help us obtain that final, perfect, eternal bliss with God. But what are we to do in the meanwhile, as travelers here on the earth?

---

[19] Aquinas's respectful appellation for Aristotle of Stagira (384–322 BC).

[20] *ST*, I-II, Q. 3, a.2.

[21] *Confessions*, bk. 1, chap. 1.

"According to the Philosopher (*Ethic.* i, 9), happiness is the reward of works of virtue."[22] So then, to attain some measure of happiness on earth, we've got some work cut out for us—and the same applies to perfect happiness in heaven. As Jesus himself declared, "If you know these things, you shall be blessed if you do them" (John 13:17). There are things we need to *know* and to *do*—there's a place for faith and a place for works—to attain some happiness on earth and perfect, blessed happiness in heaven. Virtues are perfections of our God-given powers as human beings. To understand virtue we must understand those powers. Got a minute for Aquinas to spell out the nature of our human nature? Very good then. It's time for chapter 2.

[22] *ST*, I-II, Q. 5, art. 7.

CHAPTER TWO

What Are We?
Body and Soul.

*We shall treat first of the nature of man,
and secondly of his origin.*

—ST, I, Q. 75, prologue

Got Soul?

If we are to attain happiness, we need to find out what will truly complete and fulfill us. To discover that, we must understand just what and who we are as human beings. In his *Treatise on Man* (I, QQ. 75–102), St. Thomas Aquinas combs the Scriptures, the writings of the Church Fathers, and the best of human philosophers to arrive at fundamental truths about our humanity.

When theologians talk about human nature, they consider man's relation to his soul. What is the soul? It's not a material body. Material bodies can't do what creatures with souls can do. Go ask your pet rock about it, and see what answer you get. Even ensouled creatures can't do much on earth when the soul has left the body.

A soul is the difference between a living body and a corpse. The material is all still there, but it isn't . . . animated. (*Anima* is Latin for "soul.") That, then, is the most basic function of the soul. It is the first principle of life.

So the soul really matters. But speaking of matter, how can the human soul be immaterial, that is, spiritual, and yet so intrinsically linked to our material bodies? Well, it's a matter of matter and form. Aquinas, echoing and expanding on Aristotle, recognized that humans are composite, hylomorphic beings (from the Greek *hyle*, for "matter" and *morphe*, for "form"). Our bodies are "matter," and our souls are "form."

What is the matter with form?

Some great thinkers, such as Plato, believed that men, in essence, are spiritual souls trapped in material bodies while on earth. Others, such as Democritus in ancient times and many people today who consider themselves scientific, believe we are nothing but matter, and that the soul is an old-fashioned fiction. Aquinas could not disagree more with both of those views. He says the body and soul are a composite unity. Aristotle had tersely noted fifteen hundred years earlier, "We can dismiss the question of whether the soul and body are one; it is as though we were to ask whether the wax and its shape are one."[23]

Thomas gives the question a thorough answer. He notes, "Matter is that which is not as such 'a particular thing,' but is in mere potency to become a 'particular thing.' Form is that by which a 'particular thing' actually exists. And the compound is the 'particular thing' itself."[24]

---

[23] *On the Soul*, bk. 2, chap. 12; cited in Jonathan Barnes, ed., *The Complete Works of Aristotle* (Princeton, NJ: Princeton University Press, 1984), 657.

[24] *Aquinas's Commentary on De Anima* (*On the Soul*), bk. 2, chap. 1; cited in Thomas S. Hibbs, ed. *Aquinas on Human Nature* (Indianapolis, IN: Hackett Publishing Co., 1999), 19.

The soul is the form of the body—that which makes us particular human beings.[25]

A word about perfection, which St. Thomas uses in a specific way: to be perfect is literally to be complete. In Latin, *per* + *factus* means "thoroughly made." God is perfect in that he is complete in every attribute. Thomas says that in matter, there are four degrees of perfection: 1) existence, 2) living, 3) sensing, and 4) understanding. As living human beings, you and I reach all four. Your pet rock has attained only the first degree, which in itself is good—for as Thomas will make clear in Part II, "all that exists is good." And yet the rock can't do much more than sit there, because it does not have a soul. But does your tomato plant have a soul? St. Thomas would answer an unequivocal yes!

How does your tomato plant differ from your pet rock?

We sometimes call nonliving things at that first level of perfection inanimate objects, and living things at the next three levels animate objects. This makes perfect sense to St. Thomas, because, as we said, *anima* means "soul." Your tomato plant is (or was) living, so it does (or did) have a soul—a vegetative soul. How perfectly fitting for a vegetable. Perhaps you've heard of the "fruit or vegetable" controversy surrounding the tomato. To scientists it is a fruit because it develops in the ovaries of the plant's flower, and to cooks it is a vegetable, because it is used in savory cooking, not sweet. St. Thomas doesn't give a hoot about those differences. Fruits, vegetables, trees, bushes, your

[25] This is the official teaching of the Church as well. See the *Catechism of the Catholic Church*, no. 365.

front lawn, and any kind of plant life all possess a vegetative soul. That soul's powers are three: 1) nutrition, 2) growth, and 3) reproduction.

But what about your dog or cat? Fido and Tinkerbell certainly don't spend all their time sitting in one spot, simply eating, growing, and reproducing like plants. They have a higher type of soul, which St. Thomas calls sensitive. They can see, hear, touch, taste, and smell. They know what they like. They have appetites that attract them to things, and legs and paws that get them those things — in some cases, to gobble them up or reproduce with them. (Notice that every higher kind of soul contains the powers of the lower souls, and then some.) In other words, Fido, Tinkerbell, and all animal life possess the powers of sensation, appetites, and locomotion, in addition to all the vegetative powers of your tomato plant.

But what about you and me? Since you are reading this book, I'm willing to wager that you possess an even higher type of soul, the kind made for understanding. I'm willing to wager as well that it's not just your soul that is reading this book. (Close your eyes and try reading with just your soul. Any luck?)

What you share with dogs and cats

If you're paying close attention, you have deduced that you and your pets share in the vegetative and sensitive powers of the soul. You all have the vegetative capacities for nutrition, growth, and reproduction, along with all the sensitive capacities of the five senses, and the powers to move about and to desire to obtain some things and avoid others. You'll also have to admit that Fido and Tinkerbell probably outdo you in at least a few of those powers; for example, in smelling and hearing. But there is more to the story.

We'll flesh this all out in entries ahead, but let's note for now that the appetites we share with animals are of two kinds: the *concupiscible* appetite refers to the capacity to desire and seek out good things, while the *irascible* appetite refers to the capacity to get all riled up, literally to raise the "ire," to fight off or flee from bad things that would cause harm.

As for the senses, do you realize that those five exterior senses we share (touch, sight, hearing, smell, and taste) and which are made possible by the bodily organs of the skin, eyes, ears, nose, and tongue, are accompanied by four more interior senses—brought to us courtesy of our brains? We also share these interior senses, in a manner, with other animals. They are the common sense, imagination, memory, and the estimative sense. These fascinating capacities are shared in a manner with other animals because, although they have similar functions and achieve similar things, in other animals they operate largely on auto-pilot, guided by instinct. In human beings, they are amenable to override by the rational, willful, intellectual soul. It's the soul that makes all the difference. Now let's see what difference it makes.

CHAPTER THREE

What Does a Soul Do?

*Although man is of the same genus as
other animals, he is of a different species.*

— ST, I, Q. 75, art. 3

How do we differ from Fido and Tinkerbell?

The human soul is unique in the known universe. We eat, grow,
and reproduce, as does any old tomato. We also taste, touch,
hear, smell, see, and move about, much like Fido and Tinkerbell. But there is something very special about us. Our souls give
us powers to understand, to name, to define, to classify, and to
communicate our understanding to others. No other earthly,
ensouled creatures can do this because only we have immaterial, spiritual, *intellectual souls.*

Having an intellectual soul is a very important thing indeed,
because it is through this gift that we are made in the image and
likeness of God. Unlike plants, we are not bound to know and
live only through things that come into physical contact with
our bodies. Unlike dogs or cats, we are not bound to the individual particular objects that we can see, hear, taste, touch, or
smell. We can also conceptualize and speak of "dogs" and "cats"
as groups and of much higher, nonmaterial, abstract concepts —
such as justice, love, knowledge, truth, beauty, goodness, and

God. Like God, but in an infinitely more limited sense, we have the power to know and understand realities beyond the world of the senses. Further, not only do we have *intellect*; we also have *will*. Animals have powerful desires and powerful muscles and weapons to take what they want (or to prevent themselves from being taken). But their actions are guided by instincts, while we can decide the goals we will or will not pursue, guided by our intellectual powers of reasoning. We are able to know the difference between right and wrong and to know that some good things must be left alone in deference to higher goods.

What do our senses tell us?

Like animals, our awareness of the world comes to us from our senses. Material objects in the world are composites consisting of matter and form. Matter, for St. Thomas as for Aristotle before him, refers to a thing's potency or potential for being that is actualized by the essential nature that is its form. A material cause is that out of which something is made. A formal cause is that into which something is made. As we have already seen, for living beings, matter and form are body and soul.

Now, vegetables do not think. (At least, I don't think they do.) Beings with a vegetative soul interact with the world by taking in matter and form, as when plants absorb water and nutrients from the soil. We do the same when we eat. Animals, however, with the powers of sensitive souls, are able to take in the forms of objects without their matter. When we eat an apple, it's gone, but when we see it, touch it, or smell it, we take in its form — information about what it is — without consuming its matter. Everything we come to know about that apple, whether or not we decide to gobble it down, starts with the information we derive from our five senses. Some thinkers, such as Plato, believed that we are born with innate ideas about things. St. Thomas argued that we are born a blank slate—*tabula rasa*, in the familiar Latin phrase.

So where do our thoughts come from? They come to us first from our senses, as we detect sensations, sights, sounds, odors, and tastes in the outside world (and at times from within our own bodies). The same can be said for Fido and Tinkerbell, but we are just getting started, and they are much closer to reaching the end of their powers to know. Let's trace the path to our thoughts now a little further, and see where we and other animals come to a definitive fork in the road—the road to understanding.

The riddle of the senses

I see a patch of white, hear a flapping sound, feel dampness, smell a musty odor, and taste a hint of salt. Whatever could it be? My senses have not told me much else. Now I perceive that it's something hardly a few inches tall, is just a few inches from me, is nearly as round as it is wide, has four downward tubular projections and one in the back that is moving quickly from side to side. Still don't know what it is? Then let me introduce you to our new puppy, Lily. She has just come in from the rain, and she's shaking herself dry.

Note how the disparate bits of information coming in from our separate external senses don't necessarily make much sense until they are all put together and integrated by what St. Thomas called the *sensus communis* or "common sense." He is not talking about the kind of practical, down-to-earth, common sense that your parents always encouraged you to use, but a special, synthesizing power of the human soul. It is this common sense that allows us to perceive as one thing the many data provided by our external senses. In modern psychological terminology, the senses produce sensation, but the common sense — the first of what St. Thomas calls the four internal senses, produces perception. Perception derives from the Latin word *percipere*, "to seize wholly" (as a whole, unified thing — in this case, our new puppy, Lily).

So the common sense does indeed make sense, but so do three other internal senses. I'll bet you've formed some kind of mental image of little Lily, haven't you? To help you a bit, she's a ten-week-old miniature American Eskimo puppy. She's pure lily white, like a little furry snowball. As I write, she's not much over four pounds. That mental image you have now formed is courtesy of a second internal sense — called, quite appropriately, *imagination*. Aristotle believed that "the soul never thinks without an image,"[26] and the Angelic Doctor agreed.

Imagination, memory, and the cogitative sense

All animals have the power to hold on to sense perceptions after the object that produced them is no longer there to act on the sense organs. This basic power of forming images[27] is called imagination. These re-presentations of original experiences free us from the confines of the immediate present. The imagination also has another, very imaginative trick up its sleeve: its ability to combine and form images of things that we have never experienced. None of us has ever seen a puppy the size of an elephant,[28] but we can easily enough imagine a gigantic Lily. (Since she's in the teething phase, it is happily but a figment of

[26] *On the Soul*, III, 7.
[27] "Phantasms" in Aristotle's Greek, deriving from a word meaning "light."
[28] *Clifford, the Big Red Dog* children's books notwithstanding.

the imagination.) Images are, nonetheless, the building blocks of our thoughts.

A third internal sense is memory. It builds up those powers of imagination with temporal, emotional, and intellectual components. Through the power of memory, we realize that the objects of our images are not only absent, but they happened in the past. Our personal memories are also embedded in the context of the emotional experiences in which they occurred. Call to mind your grandma or your best childhood friend, and you are likely to feel something too. And for human beings, the intellect also comes into play. Courtesy of powers we'll describe in the pages ahead, not only can we hold on to past impressions via sensory memory, as do other animals, but we possess powers of recollection, whereby we can use our thinking powers to figure out strategies for recalling old things and remembering new ones.

Last of the four is the cogitative sense. Not only do we perceive things as having certain sensible qualities; we have a sense of whether they are good or bad for us. In animals it comes from instinct; in man, particular reason comes into play.

The secret of the agent:
do you have an *agent intellect*?

This is where we and animals like Fido, Tinkerbell, and Lily must part ways, since man alone possesses, not merely a sensitive, but an intellectual soul. The thinking of animals stops at the level of phantasms or images. These images capture and re-present particular things and events or particular dogs, such as Lily, for example. We, however, can speak of dogs in general too. You have probably never met Lily, but you understand what I mean when I talk about her. In fact, as for all of the words I use in this book, you either understand them, or if you don't, you possess the capacity to ask someone what they mean or to look them up somewhere. Lily and all other animal species produce no words at all. Human beings can also talk about abstractions such as truth, justice, and the American way, even though we can't actually see, hear, touch, taste, or smell them. This is the gift of the intellectual soul, and it possesses two main powers.

Just as the internal senses produce images from sense impressions, the agent intellect produces abstractions from those images. The Latin word *intellectus* derives from *intus* ("inside") and *legere* ("to read"). The agent intellect looks below the surface of experience to abstract ("draw forth") the essences of objects that have stimulated our senses. It sorts the jumble of sensory data to perceive a thing's essential, universal nature. The agent intellect's gaze is unobstructed by particular, accidental features; it's like an X-ray that looks through the externals to see the reality below the appearance. My eyes look at little Lily and giant Enzo, the ninety-pound golden retriever who lives next door, and my agent intellect detects the quiddity—the "whatness," or in this case, the "dog-ness"—that they share.

But the intellect has not finished its workings on their white or golden furriness.

Mission possible: what is the possible intellect?

The abstraction produced by the agent intellect is immaterial, and is not the product of any particular bodily organs, as the products of the senses are. The last stop on the road to human understanding is the *possible* intellect. Just as the percepts of the senses and common sense provide that data for images, the abstractions of the agent intellect provide the fodder for the ideas or concepts of the possible intellect. The abstraction then is received by the powers of the possible intellect, which stimulates it to produce a product of its own, which we call a concept or idea.[29] Get the idea? Maybe this will help:

The Birth of an Idea

Faculties	Outer sense and common sense ↓	Imagination Memory Cogitative sense	Agent intellect	Possible intellect
Product	→ *Percept* →	*Phantasm* →	*Abstraction* →	*Concept or idea*
Description	Impressed sensible species	Expressed sensible species	Impressed intelligible species	Expressed intelligible species

Adapted from Robert E. Brennan, *Thomistic Psychology* (New York: Macmillan, 1941), 183.

[29] Many modern philosophers since the days of John Locke cast doubt on the powers of the mind by supposing that ideas are the objects of our thinking or *that which we think about*, thus severing the direct connection between our ideas and the outside world. St. Thomas makes clear that objects themselves are the objects of our ideas and our ideas are primarily a means or *that by which we think about things*, although we *also* possess the self-reflective capacity to think about our thinking, when we are so inclined.

Do our thoughts live forever?

Let's note that as we move along the road to human understanding, we start with *particular things* and end with *universal ideas*. We start with the sensations produced by *material*, bodily organs and end with concepts of a purely *spiritual*, intellectual soul. In sensations, forms are separated from matter, but not from the conditions of particular material things: if you *see* a rock, you see it because it's sitting in front of you. In the ideas of the intellect, forms are separated from matter and from its particular conditions as well: if you're *thinking* about a rock, your mind "sees" it, whether it's in front of you or not. Sensations are particular and concrete; ideas are universal and abstract.

Since the intellect can potentially know the essence of *all* material bodies, it cannot itself be a material organ.[30] As Thomas points out, "if the intellectual soul were composed of matter and form, the forms of things would be received into it as individuals, and so it would only know the individual; just as it happens with the sensitive powers which receive forms in a corporal organ; since matter is the principle by which forms are individualized. It follows, therefore, that the intellectual soul—and every intellectual substance which has knowledge of forms absolutely—is exempt from composition of matter and form."[31]

---

[30] Since humans are soul-body composites, the soul is indeed supplied with phantasms by bodily organs such as the sense organs, which send information to our brains. Thus, damage to those material organs can hinder the spiritual intellect in forming new ideas and performing other intellectual operations such as judgment and reasoning, which we will describe in due course.

[31] *ST*, I, Q. 75, art. 5.

What Does a Soul Do?

We'll flesh out (actually unflesh, so to speak) this idea later on. For now, let's note one other important implication of the immateriality of the human intellectual soul — in fact, it's the most important of all possible implications. Because the human soul is *immaterial*, it has no parts that can decompose. Barring an act of annihilation from God himself, *the soul is also immortal*. How important it is, then, to act in ways pleasing to the God who breathed immortality into our spiritual souls!

Some Powers of the Human Soul

Vegetative Soul

Nutrition	Growth	Reproduction

Sensitive Soul

Touch	Common sense	Concupiscence
Taste	Imagination	Irascibility
Smell	Memory	
Hearing	Cogitative sense	Locomotion
Vision		

Intellectual Soul

Agent intellect	Possible intellect	Will

DUMB OX BOX #1
Is it a sin to be boring?

Indeed it can be, if you strive to bore others — or if you simply take no care to avoid it! We'd best hear St. Thomas himself on this one: "In human affairs whatever is against reason is a sin. Now, it is against reason for a man to be burdensome to others, by offering no pleasure to others, and by hindering their enjoyment."

Further, he points out: "A man who is without mirth, not only is lacking playful speech, but is also burdensome to others, since he is deaf to the moderate mirth of others" (*ST*, II-II, Q. 168, art. 4).

Clearly, then, the Angelic Doctor would not have us be party poopers! He knew well that all work and no play indeed makes us dull boys and girls (and in a venial sense, even sinful ones). Let us do our duty and spread good cheer with joyous and "moderate mirth"!

CHAPTER FOUR

Ruled by a Free Will

Since therefore Happiness is to be gained
by means of certain acts, we must in due sequence
consider human acts, in order to know
by what acts we may obtain Happiness, and
by what acts we are prevented from obtaining it.

—*ST*, I-II, Q. 6, prologue

We've seen how the intellectual powers of the human soul are unique among all creatures on earth. Being composites of material bodies and spiritual souls, we have a uniquely human way of knowing that is inaccessible to irrational animals. Angels have higher intellects. As purely spiritual beings, their knowledge of what things are comes all at once to them as instantaneous intuition. They don't require sensory data and the multiple steps of cognitive processing and reasoning that we do.[32] Human beings not only have a unique way of *knowing*; we have a unique way of *acting* as well.

If we want to know which human acts lead to happiness, we must learn about the human *will*. And since there's a will, you

---

[32] Readers intrigued by angels will delight in the Angelic Doctor's treatise about them: *ST*, I-I, QQ. 50-64.

can rest assured that St. Thomas has provided a *way* to understand it.

Questions 1–21 in the First Part of the Second Part of the *Summa Theologica* address such issues of human acts, taking more than a hundred pages to do so. With only a few minutes, we'll give you the highlights in a bit over three pages.

Will and *free* will: there's a difference![33]

Voluntas—the will—is a uniquely human power. It's such an important subject in understanding our freedom and our salvation that St. Thomas uses the word in ways that are more exacting than our colloquial understanding of will as "whatever I happen to want at the moment." So hang on for the ride—it's worth it.

As the intellect seeks to know the *true*, the will seeks to obtain the *good*. The intellect operates in the realm of *knowledge*, and the will in the realm of *love*. The intellect *discerns* what is good, and the will *acts* to get it. The will is *the capacity to desire what is truly good*. Hold on! In the everyday sense, we know that we *can* desire the truly good—but we don't always pursue it. But first things first: Without a will, we couldn't even desire it.

Since the ultimate *end* of man is the attainment of happiness, there is a sense in which the will itself is not free, since no one can truly desire unhappiness. Augustine says, "All desire happiness with one will," and Thomas agrees, saying, "The will desires something of necessity."[34] This does not mean, as some modern deterministic psychologists and philosophers hold, that

---

[33] St. Thomas introduces will and free-will in Part I, QQ. 82 and 83 and expands his treatment starting with I-II, Q. 6.

[34] *ST*, I, Q. 82, art. 1.

we have no free will, that our acts are determined for us and are not our responsibility. Indeed, Thomas retorts to deniers of free will, "*I answer that,* Man has free will: otherwise counsels, exhortations, commands, prohibitions, rewards and punishments would be in vain."[35]

If the will is *necessitated* to desire the good, how, then, can we have *free* will? Thomas says that the "proper act" of free will is *choice*. We have *freedom of exercise* to choose whether to employ our wills and make a choice one way or another in a given situation. (Surely procrastinators can relate to this!) We have *freedom of specification* to select one thing or course of action while rejecting others. Our free choice is not in regard to the end or goal: We want happiness. What we choose is the *means to that end.* It is through our ability to choose or not to choose between different means that we exercise free will and become active, nondetermined agents — masters of our own actions and worthy of praise or of blame.

Willpower: on becoming what we think about

St. James tells us, "Every man is tempted by his own concupiscence, being drawn away and allured" (James 1:14). Even St. Paul laments, "For I do not that good which I will; but the evil which I hate, that I do" (Rom. 7:15). Surely, every one of us can attest to the truth of these words. Our desires ever remind us that the human *intellectual* soul possesses within it all of the passions and desires of our *sensitive* souls as well. Through the reasoning powers of the intellect, the will is presented with what is morally right and truly good for us. Our sensual appetites can tempt us powerfully toward wrongful things that may

[35] *ST*, I, Q. 83, art. 1.

provide some immediate pleasure or satisfaction, but will harm us or others in the long run. How can we build the "will power" to do the right thing consistently?

To make a long story short,[36] we need to realize that the will (the rational appetite) does not rule over concupiscible and irascible powers (sensitive appetites) like a despotic king, as a master to his slaves. The will is more like a political governor whose citizens can act counter to his commands. So, one key to doing the good that we want is to fix our intellects on the things that motivate our will to command the right choices. We need to keep our eyes on the prize — to saturate our minds with lofty goals, with the words of Scripture and with prayerful conversation with God. When we train ourselves to become mindful of higher goods, the lesser goods of the world seem less enticing and have less impact on us.

Twentieth-century motivational speaker Earl Nightingale put it, "We become what we think about." He called this "the strangest secret." If we would become the best that we can be, the wisdom of St. Thomas must not remain a secret. We all need to think about it!

---

[36] To make this short story long and complete, we'll examine this question from nearly every possible angle when we address the virtues in general and specific virtues in the pages ahead, for that is virtue's job.

CHAPTER FIVE

Your Soul and Its Eleven Passions

*Augustine says (De Civ. Dei, xiv. 7, 9)
that all the passions are caused by love.*

—*ST*, I-II, Q. 25, art. 2,
citing Augustine's *City of God*

When we hear of "passion" today, we are likely to think of intense erotic desire or perhaps of an obsessive ambition to participate in some activity—such as "a passion" for one's work, a sport, a particular sports car, or a special hobby or interest. These meanings capture only part of what St. Thomas calls "the passions." Thomas calls passions what we commonly refer to as feelings or emotions. Even though we experience them intensely and they may motivate us to action, Thomas uses the word passion because the word implies *passivity*, in the sense that our bodies and souls have *receptivity*—the ability to be influenced by objects outside ourselves, whether to draw us toward them (as in love) or repel us (as in hate).

Stones don't have passions and neither do trees, but our pets and the beasts in the wild do, and so do we. *The passions are movements of the sensitive appetites of the soul when we are faced with good or evil.* You will recall that we have two primary sensitive appetites: the *concupiscible* appetite, fueled by *love*, whereby we have affinity for the good and are repelled by evil; and the *irascible* appetite, which motivates us to remove difficult obstacles to the attainment of what we love. In the last analysis, love conquers all, since even the passions of the irascible appetite ultimately strive to remove whatever evils come between us and that which we love. But it's time now for a "first analysis," to break down these passions in us.

Do you know *your* eleven passions?

Here are the passions, in order.

We are made for what's good. Indeed, we love and desire it with our *concupiscible* appetite. This affinity, this "certain inclination, aptitude, or connaturalness in respect of the good,"[37] is called *love* (1), and it is the overruling human (and animal) passion. When some good we have perceived has not yet been attained, we experience that bittersweet passion called *desire* (2)—sweet because it is directed toward the object of our love, bitter because it is beyond our reach. When we have finally attained the good that we seek, we rest in a state of *joy* (3). Thank God that we are all ultimately made to rest in the ultimate joy that he brings. We have a natural inclination to love the good and to *hate* (4) what is evil. When the evil has not yet been experienced, we feel an *aversion* (5) or dislike for it; when we experience an already present evil, we experience sadness or *sorrow* (6). When difficulties lie between us and the good that we seek, our irascible appetites are called into play. We experience that positive feeling of *hope* (7) when we believe that the good is attainable and the bleak-

[37] *ST*, I-II, Q. 23, art. 4.

ness of *despair* (8) when we see obstacles as insurmountable. When we perceive that a difficult evil may be conquered, we experience the passion of *daring* (9), and when we believe we are not up to the task of conquering an evil, we experience *fear* (10). When we have already experienced a difficult evil, it raises the ire of our irascible appetite with the passion of *anger* (11).

These potentially powerful passions can spell the difference between happiness and misery, between mental health and distress. After we review all eleven, let's take a minute to see what *practical advice* St. Thomas can offer *to us* for alleviating sorrow, fear, despair, and anger.

How can we succor sorrow?

St. Thomas can offer us practical wisdom for dealing with troublesome passions, partly because he so well grasps the implications of the fact that we are ensouled, mind-body unities. In prescribing "the remedies of sorrow or pain,"[38] he notes that when we have experienced an evil in the form of a loss or negative event of some kind, we can lessen our distress by 1) experiencing pleasures of some kind, 2) weeping, 3) experiencing the sympathy of friends, 4) contemplating the truth, and indeed, even by 5) sleep and baths!

Thomas tells us that "pleasure is to sorrow, what, in bodies, repose is to weariness"[39]—it helps counteract it. He notes that when Augustine mourned the death of his friend, "*in groans and in tears alone did he find some little refreshment.*"[40] In weeping, our focus is moved from our self-enclosed thoughts toward outward

[38] *ST*, I-II, Q. 38.
[39] Ibid.
[40] Ibid.

The Eleven Passions of Man

Passion	Object	Definition
Love	Good	Affinity for the good.
Desire	Good	Attraction toward a good not yet attained.
Joy	Good	Rest in the good attained.
Hatred	Evil	Revulsion from evil.
Aversion	Evil	Repulsion from evil not yet experienced.
Sorrow	Evil	Succumbing to evil already present.
Hope	Arduous good	Attraction toward the attainable, but difficult good.
Despair	Arduous good	Attraction toward the unattainable, difficult good.
Daring	Arduous evil	Revulsion from conquerable, difficult evil.
Fear	Arduous evil	Revulsion from unconquerable, difficult evil.
Anger	Arduous evil	Revulsion from difficult evil already experienced.

Concupiscible Appetite (Love–Sorrow); Irascible Appetite (Hope–Anger)

actions. Also, because groans and tears are fitting actions to that state of passion, they produce a kind of pleasure.

The sympathy of friends also works in a twofold manner. First, since sorrow depresses and weighs us down, when friends share our sorrows, it is as if they share our burdens and lessen the weight. Further, a friend's condolences show his love for us, and this is a source of great pleasure. When we contemplate the truth, we move from the realm of the passions to the realm of the intellectual soul. When we read in James (1:2), "Count it all joy, my brethren, when you fall into divers temptations," we see how the contemplation of our future happiness with God can diminish any sorrow.

So much for the soul. As to the body, Augustine wrote that "the bath had its name[41]. . . from the fact of its driving sadness from the mind." Ambrose reported, "Sleep restores the tired limbs to labor, refreshes the weary mind, and banishes sorrow."

Can we kiss anger goodbye?

Sometimes. We see Thomas's integrated view of matter and spirit, body and soul, most clearly in his treatment of anger. He notes that some describe anger as "a kindling of the blood around the heart," that a "disposition to anger is due to a bilious temperament," and yet "anger arises from an emotion of the soul due to the wrong inflicted."[42] It's interesting that he touches on anger's connection with the heart, given that some modern research on people with the driven, type A personality indicates that those most prone to heart attacks have a tendency toward frequent bouts of anger. Anger is dangerous be-

[41] *Balneum*, from the Greek Βαλανεῖον.
[42] *ST*, I-II, Q. 22, art. 2; Q. 46, arts. 5, 6.

cause it can cloud reason. But anger is not always a bad thing, since it can motivate acts to redress wrongs. Aquinas agreed with Aristotle that anger must be directed at the right person, in the right manner, at the right time, and for the right reason.

As Christians, we are called to control our anger, but a far more grievous fault is hatred. Thomas tells us, "Augustine, in his Rule, compares hatred to *a beam*, but anger to *a mote*."[43] When we are *angry*, we wish some evil upon someone who has intentionally slighted or harmed us in some way, but with a sense of righteous indignation and in the pursuit of justice. If we perceive that our anger has exceeded the bounds of justice, we will then show mercy to the person who has offended us. But when we *hate* another person, we wish evil to him *as evil* and will exceed the bounds of justice without relenting. "The Philosopher says (*Rhet.* ii, 4) that the angry man is appeased if many evils befall, whereas the hater is never appeased" and that "hatred is more incurable than anger." The Angelic Doctor concurs: "Hatred is far worse and graver than anger."[44] Hatred opposes the charitable love of neighbor that Christ expects of us.

[43] *ST*, I-II, Q. 46, art. 6 (cf. Matt. 7:3).
[44] Ibid., citing Aristotle's *Rhetoric*, ii, 7.

CHAPTER SIX

The Habits That Shape Your Soul

*Every power which may be variously
directed to act needs a habit whereby
it is well disposed to its act.*

—*ST*, I-II, Q. 50, art. 5

Our human natures give rise to all sorts of capacities or powers
to operate in the realms of knowing, feeling, and doing, but
are we making the most of them? Listen to twentieth-century
American psychologist and philosopher William James, who
literally wrote the book on *Habit*: "Compared to what we ought
to be, we are only half awake. Our fires are damped, our drafts
are checked. We are using only a small part of our physical and
mental resources."[45] I feel certain that thirteenth-century psychologist and philosopher St. Thomas Aquinas, who wrote the
Treatise on Habits,[46] would heartily agree with the notion, and
with the prescription for waking ourselves up and firing up our
souls to seek their physical and spiritual perfection.

---

[45] William James, *The Energies of Men* (New York: Moffat, Yard,
and Company, 1914), 14.
[46] *ST*, I-II, QQ. 49–54.

Most theological treatises on moral behavior before and during St. Thomas's era focused on *sin*, on man's abject weakness and his inability to take any real action to perfect himself. Many of those theologians, like modern Freudian "depth psychologists," had great interest in understanding *how low we can go*. But Thomas was more interested in learning *how high we can rise*. He noted that although we cannot perfect ourselves or obtain perfect happiness without the grace of God, God does expect some cooperation on our part! We need to *consent* to his *supernatural graces* and also to put forth *effort* to perfect the *natural powers* he has graced us with. This we do, by building good and godly *habits*.

The force of habits

"The word *habitus* (habit) derives from the word *habere* (to have)."[47] This implies that habits are something relatively stable, things we have that stay with us over time. Habits are stable *dispositions*, which incline us to act in certain ways, for well or ill, and they can be found in body as well as in soul. In the realm of the body, health, beauty, and strength can be habits, as can sickness, ugliness, and weakness. As individuals, we have different inborn dispositions or potentials in different powers. We cannot all become the world's strongest man or the world's most beautiful woman, but we can establish habitual behaviors that will move us toward or away from greater strength or beauty, for "a disposition becomes a habit, just as a boy becomes a man."[48]

As important as habits of health and fitness may be, habits of the soul are of even greater importance. As the apostle St.

---

[47] *ST*, I-II, Q. 49, art. 1.
[48] Ibid., art. 2.

Paul put it: "Exercise thyself unto godliness. For bodily exercise is profitable to little: but godliness is profitable to all things, having promise of the life that now is, and of that which is to come" (1 Tim. 4:7-8).

Training to produce godliness begins with purposely building good habits that will make the most of our natural powers. Even more importantly, it entails accepting God's grace in accepting the supernatural habits we'll need to attain the theological virtues. Godly habits will dispose our various appetitive, rational, and volitional powers to act in accordance with right reason and with the will of God. These habits will perfect our particular powers, such as the concupiscible and irascible appetites, the intellect, and the will. When good habits are established, they become "second nature," making it natural, easy, and pleasurable to do the right things. So how do we build good habits?

Getting better habits

"A habit of virtue cannot be caused by one act, but only by many."[49] Good habits are built by repeated actions. As Aristotle noted, "We become builders by building and harpists by playing the harp."[50] The habit of physical strength illustrates this most clearly. The weightlifter who would make himself strong must return to the gym again and again over time, each training session contributing some small part to the strength he will eventually attain. But not every act of a power will increase the strength of a habit. "If, however, the act falls short of the intensity of the habit, such an act does not dispose to an

[49] *ST*, I-II, Q. 51, art. 3.
[50] *Nichomachean Ethics*, bk. 2.

increase of the habit, but rather to a lessening thereof."[51] If the weightlifter chooses to lift lighter weights, if the seasoned pianist plays tunes only from primers, if the philosopher reads only supermarket tabloids, their habits of physical strength, musical virtuosity, or intellectual wisdom will gradually decline. To the contrary, the wise weightlifter, musician, or philosopher will strive to increase progressively the intensity of his habitual acts, heaving heavier weights, playing more challenging pieces, and reading ever deeper tomes (like the *Summa Theologica*).

So, although habits are things that we have, they can be lost. Modern research has shown time and again that the best advice to maintain maximum physical health and mental functioning as we age is to "use it or lose it." And St. Thomas heartily concurs, noting, "Virtue is destroyed or lessened through cessation from act."[52] Perhaps you've noted as well that we can hardly speak about habit without the word *virtue* popping up. That's all for the better, since virtue is the stuff of our very next chapter.

[51] *ST*, I-II, Q. 52, art. 3.
[52] *ST*, I-II, Q. 53, art. 3.

CHAPTER SEVEN

Virtue: The Power to Do Good

Virtue denotes a certain perfection of a power.

—*ST*, I-II, Q. 55, art.1

Virtue — Gateway to the Good

We saw that habits direct our various human powers to their acts. Good habits direct us toward good acts, and another word for a *good habit* is a *virtue*.[53] Our word *virtue* derives from the Latin *vir* for "man," because virtues perfect us as human beings. As Aristotle wrote, "Virtue is that which makes its possessor good, and his work good likewise."[54]

"Yes," you reply, "but Aristotle wrote in Greek, not Latin." True. The ancient Greek word for virtue is *arete*, or "excellence." This sense is carried over in Thomas's description of virtues as *perfections* of our powers—powers like our intellects, wills, and appetites.

When we possess virtues, it becomes easier, more natural, and more enjoyable for us to do the right things. We're able to maximize our powers. Those fundamental powers include the

---

[53] Bad habits are *vices*. (Stay tuned for our next chapter.)
[54] *Ethics*, ii, 6; cited in *ST*, I-II, Q. 56, art. 1.

ability to *desire* and to *will*, to discern what we seek to enjoy or to avoid, and to *choose freely* whether we will pursue those desires. Since our natures are fallen, our desires themselves are no sure guides to the excellence and happiness that come from perfecting our powers and aiming them toward the right ends. As men with rational, intellectual powers, our choices must be guided by *right reason* to be virtuous. As *Christians*, our choices must be guided by the precepts of the *faith* as well.[55]

What are the virtues of nature?

Natural virtues were known to the great pagan philosophers and appear in Scripture as well.[56] The seeds of these virtues are planted in our human nature from birth, and they can thrive or wither through our efforts or lack thereof. They help us counteract and conquer the vices that arise from the sinful side of our fallen nature. They are composed of "moral virtues," directed toward *doing* good, and perhaps a lesser-known group of "intellectual virtues" that help us to *know* what is good.

The most fundamental *moral virtues* have been known as the *cardinal virtues*, since they "are about those things upon which human life is chiefly occupied, just as a door turns upon a hinge."[57] (*Cardo* is Latin for "hinge.")

---

[55] The *Catechism of the Catholic Church* addresses the virtues in its section on "Life in Christ" (nos. 1803–1805).

[56] For example: "And if anyone loves righteousness, her labors are virtues: for she teaches self-control and prudence, justice and courage; nothing in life is more profitable to men than these" (Wisd. 8:7, RSV), and "By wisdom a house is built, and by understanding it is established; by knowledge the rooms are filled with all precious and pleasant riches." (Prov. 24:3–4, RSV).

[57] *ST*, II-II, Q. 123, art. 7.

Temperance perfects our capacity to control our concupiscible appetite to seek what is truly good.

Fortitude perfects our capacity to harness our irascible appetite to do battle with that which would keep us from the good.

Justice perfects the capacity of our will to seek and do good not only for ourselves, but to render everyone his rightful due.

Prudence perfects our ability to determine the proper means to achieve the good and to act upon it.

Vice: too much (or too little) of a good thing

Aristotle's conception of virtue has been called "the golden mean." "Nothing in excess" was a related Greek maxim inscribed in the forecourt of the Temple to Apollo at Delphi. It means that virtue lies between the vices of the extremes — between deficiency on one side and excess on the other. But perhaps the mean, or middle, also conveys to you the suggestion of compromise or of mediocrity. Should we be virtuous, then, but not too virtuous? No, the "mean" here does not mean going halfway. Aristotle (let alone St. Thomas!) would not have us join the lukewarm who will be spit out![58] The golden mean at which the cardinal virtues aim is not compromise between virtue and vice. Think of it as a golden peak of excellence that towers above deficiency and excess. If we are to be fully awake, with fires undamped and blazing toward perfection, we will keep our eyes fixed upon this golden peak at all times.

[58] Apoc. 3:16.

41

Just what is the mean, the action that is just right — not too little or too much? It can vary with the circumstances. It is up to us to exercise our powers of reasoning to find those means, and through repeated virtuous actions, to train ourselves in virtuous habits.

The Golden Mean

Vices of Deficiency	The Golden Mean	Vices of Excess
Foolishness	Prudence	Craftiness
Insensibility	Temperance	Profligacy
Personal loss	Justice	Personal gain
Cowardice	Fortitude	Rashness

Do our minds have virtues of their own?

Moral virtues enable us to steer our will and passions toward *doing* the good, while *intellectual* virtues enable us to *know* what is good. Aquinas, after Aristotle, describes three virtues of the *speculative intellect,* which is the intellect as it seeks and reflects upon pure truths without immediate practical considerations; and two virtues of the *practical intellect,* which is the intellect as it seeks truths that are useful for making or doing things.

The speculative-intellectual virtues are *understanding,* which is a habit of comprehending principles, of grasping essences, of forming concepts — of "penetrating into the heart of things," as we saw in chapter 2; *science* (that is, *knowledge,* from the Latin *scire,* "to know"), which is the habit of reasoning from fundamental principles about the causes, effects, and relationships

The Natural Virtues

	Power	Virtue
Intellectual	Speculative intellect	Understanding Science Wisdom
	Practical intellect	Art Prudence
Moral	Will	Justice
	Concupiscible appetite	Temperance
	Irascible appetite	Fortitude

among things; and *wisdom*, the highest of the three, which is a habit that seeks the highest causes and most important truths, judging from both the principles of understanding and the reasoned conclusions of science.

The practical intellectual virtues are *art*—which is the habit of right reason about making things, like an "artist," poet, musician, writer, architect, swordsmith, physician, et cetera—and *prudence*, a practical form of wisdom that is the habit of right reason about getting things done, through the various choices we must make in everyday life. Perhaps you've noticed that we already classed prudence as a cardinal moral virtue, and that is because it is *both* practical and intellectual. This "charioteer of the virtues"[59] functions at the intersection of the realms of

---

[59] *Catechism of the Catholic Church*, Par. 1806.

the true and the good, the intellect and the will, thought and action, the universal and the singular, the intellectual and the moral—as we'll see in chapter 13.

Are there "super" virtues?

The natural virtues pretty much exhausted the virtues known to the pagan world, although Aristotle did vaguely suggest higher "heroic" or "divine" virtues.[60] So what would "super" virtues be? *Super* is being used here as shorthand for *supernatural* virtues, which we come to know through God's revelation and experience through his *direct infusion* into our souls. They perfect us not only as *biological* beings, but as *theological* beings made in the image and likeness of God, to allow us to enjoy eternal bliss in his company. Thomas notes that limited, earthly happiness can be achieved by the natural virtues, but "the other is a happiness surpassing man's nature, and which man can obtain by the power of God alone, by a kind of participation in the Godhead, about which it is written (2 Pet. 1:4) that by Christ we are made *partakers of the Divine nature*."[61] So what are these amazing supernatural virtues?

St. Paul lists the three supernatural, *theological virtues* in his first letter to the Corinthians. "And now there remain faith, hope, and charity, these three: but the greatest of these is

---

[60] "What is the starting point of motion in the spirit? The answer then is clear; as in the universe, so there, everything is moved by God . . . and the starting point of reason is not reason but something superior to reason. What then could be superior even to knowledge and to intellect, except God?" (*Eudemian Ethics*, viii, 2. See *ST*, I-II, Q. 68, art. 1 for St. Thomas's analysis).

[61] *ST*, I-II, Q. 62, art. 1.

charity" (1 Cor. 13:13). *Faith* resides in the intellect and provides a certainty of belief in God and eternal bliss beyond what we can know through our senses and reason. *Hope* resides in the will, expressing our confidence that union with God is attainable. *Charity* (*love*) perfects the will by seeking unity with God out of simple love for him. St. Thomas describes charity as the "end" of all the virtues, the "mother" of the virtues, a "friendship with God," and our means to ultimate happiness. Faith will no longer be needed when we see God face-to-face; hope will have no role when we have already attained heaven; but the love of God will endure throughout eternity.

Anyone hungry for some gifts, blessings, and fruits?

We learn in Isaiah 11:2 of seven gifts of the Holy Spirit that the *Catechism* elaborates as "wisdom, understanding, counsel, fortitude, knowledge, piety, and fear of the Lord" (no. 1831). St. Thomas introduces them in his treatise on the virtues and notes that whereas human virtues perfect our thoughts and actions *as moved by our natural reason*, the *gifts derive from God* and perfect our thoughts and actions *as moved by the Holy Spirit*. Natural virtues are like oars with which we row toward the good. Gifts of the Holy Spirit are like God-given winds filling our sails.

Our "blessings" refer to the *beatitudes* proclaimed in Christ's Sermon on the Mount, beginning in the fifth chapter of the Gospel of St. Matthew. Jesus details these eight beatitudes, or special blessings, that come to all who display various Christlike perfections: to the poor in spirit, to those who mourn, to the meek, to those who hunger and thirst for righteousness, to the merciful, to the pure of heart, to the peacemakers, and to those who bear persecution for his sake.

God's gifts bear *fruits* as well as blessings. The Church's teachings on the fruits of the Holy Spirit build on the words of St. Paul in Galatians 5:22–23 and are found in our current *Catechism* in paragraph 1832. They are twelve in number: *charity, joy, peace, patience, kindness, goodness, generosity, gentleness, faithfulness, modesty, self-control,* and *chastity.* St. Thomas tells us, "The fruits are any virtuous deeds in which one delights." As material fruits please and refresh us, so do spiritual fruits, "with a holy and genuine delight."[62] The *gifts* make us receptive to the inspiration of God, so that we may bear (and enjoy) the *fruits.*

[62] *ST*, I-II, Q. 70, art. 1.

DUMB OX BOX #2
Is it a sin to love wine?

I sensed this question was on your mind, especially if you fancy beer, wine, or something stronger. St. Thomas has had your answer ready for more than 750 years now. He warns against excessive drinking, because it clouds our ability to reason. But he is by no means a Prohibitionist. He advises that when we drink, we should "drink to the point of hilarity." (That is, consistent with a friendly and playful lightheartedness.) The proper time, context, and situation must always be considered as well, as Scripture says: "Wine drunk in season and temperately is rejoicing of heart and gladness of soul. Wine drunk to excess is bitterness of soul with provocation and stumbling" (Ecclus. 31:28–29).

Sobriety is a virtue aligned with temperance. But virtues, you'll recall, are golden means of neither too much *nor too little*. Let's listen to Thomas on this: "If a man deliberately abstains from wine to such an extent that he does serious harm to his nature, he will not be free from blame" (*ST*, II-II, Q. 150, art. 1).

All that God made is good. He wants us to be happy and indeed playful—periodically we need to "lighten up." Now, some are prone to alcoholism and the golden mean for them may well be no alcohol at all. But St. Thomas is warning us against the *vice of deficiency* that lies beyond sobriety and involves an *insensibility* and lack of appreciation for the goodness of all God's works.

CHAPTER EIGHT

Missing the Mark:
Vice and Sin

For sin does not consist in passing from the many to the one, as is the case with virtues, which are connected, but rather in forsaking the one for the many.

—*ST*, I-II, Q. 73, art. 2

Aristotle noted that there are many ways an arrow can miss the target, as there are many ways to miss the golden mean of virtue. Because St. Thomas was the great theological champion and expositor of the virtues—of finding the means to maximize our powers of heart, mind, soul, and strength to reach our ultimate target of union with the God of love—he could not ignore the myriad sins and vices that lead us away from our target, weaken our virtue, and separate us from God.

In the *Summa Theologica*, Thomas devotes 93 pages to addressing the many sins and vices through which we lead ourselves astray. As extensive as his treatment is, it merely paves the way for his 716 pages on the theological and cardinal virtues![63]

---

[63] The stuff of chapters 11–17 in *The One-Minute Aquinas*.

The subject matter of sin and vice is very important paving nonetheless, since we must understand the many ways we can go wrong if we would train ourselves, with the grace of God, to do right. So next we'll take a look at Thomas's treatment of the ways we miss the mark, and why.

What are vice and sin?

"Augustine says (*De Perfect. Just.* ii) that vice is a quality in respect of which the soul is evil," and further, "(*De Lib. Arb.* iii): Whatever is lacking for a thing's natural perfection may be called a vice."[64] Thomas notes that as virtues are habits that make a person good, vices are habits that dispose us toward evil—evil being the lack of good. Vices are bad or evil habits as virtues are good habits. Sins are vicious acts (literally, acts of vice). Sins are to vices as good deeds are to virtues.

"That's not natural!"

"Augustine says (*De Lib. Arb.* iii, 13): *Every vice, simply because it is a vice, is contrary to nature.*"[65] Thomas notes that as man is defined by his rational, intellectual soul, since vices lead to evil, they are contrary to the nature of man as a rational animal. In other words, vices are not reasonable. Dionysius wrote that "man's good is in accordance with reason, and his evil is to be against reason." Cicero put it, "Virtue is a habit in accord with reason, like a second nature."[66] Vice, then, is a habit contrary to *reason* and to *nature*.

[64] *ST*, I-II, Q. 71, art. 1.
[65] Ibid., art. 4.
[66] Ibid., art. 2.

Vice or sin: which one's worse?

Thomas says, "A man is justly punished for a vicious act; but not for a vicious habit, so long as no act ensues. Therefore a vicious action is worse than a vicious habit."[67] It is a bad thing to develop a habit disposing oneself toward evil, but a worse thing to exercise one's will to act upon it. Indeed, by repeatedly choosing *not* to act on vicious habits, vices may be diminished.

Thought, word, or deed?

Augustine wrote: "Sin is a word, deed, or desire contrary to the eternal law."[68] Jerome too, said: "The human race is subject to three kinds of sin, for when we sin, it is either by thought, or word, or deed."[69] Thomas observes that thought (or desire), word, and deed represent three degrees or stages of sin. For example, "For the angry man, through desire of vengeance, is at first disturbed in thought, then he breaks out into words of abuse, and lastly he goes on to wrongful deeds; and the same applies to lust and to any other sin."[70]

Sin: philosophy vs. theology

Bearing in mind that sin presents barriers to the two kinds of happiness—the natural, limited happiness on earth and the perfect, eternal happiness in heaven with God—Thomas notes that "the theologian considers sin chiefly as an offense against God; and the moral philosopher as something contrary

---

[67] Ibid., art. 3.
[68] Ibid., art. 6.
[69] *ST*, I-II, Q. 72, art. 7.
[70] Ibid.

to reason."[71] Augustine defined sin as "contrary to the eternal law," rather than merely contrary to reason because "the eternal law directs us in many things that surpass human reason, e.g., in matters of faith."[72]

Carnal vs. spiritual sin: which is worse?

Sins of the flesh, like lust, are shameful sins; they offend against our own bodies, placing us on the level of animals at the mercy of their carnal desires. Spiritual sins, like pride, are worse; they employ our God-given rational powers to offend against the God who gave them.

Sins of omission or commission: which are more serious?

It seems today that we tend to consider the good things we fail to do (sins of *omission*) much less serious than the evil things we do (sins of *commission*). Thomas notes, however, that they are essentially two sides of the same coin that always appear together in some sense. When we fail to do something we know we should do—going to Sunday Mass, to take a simple example—this sin of *omission* can also be seen as a sin of *commission*, in that we *fail to* attend the Mass, because there is something else we would rather *do*. Since all sins are acts, they all imply an active turning *away* from God and a turning *to* something else. If we would grow in virtue, we need to turn away from evil *and* turn toward good. Hence, God's law has provided us with both "affirmative precepts" and "negative precepts" to follow.[73]

[71] *ST*, I-II, Q. 71, art. 6.
[72] Ibid.
[73] For example, the "Thou shalts," and "Thou shalt nots" of the Ten Commandments. See *ST*, I-II, Q. 72, art. 6.

Does the devil make us do it?

St. Thomas says, "The devil can nowise compel man to sin."[74] But we must still, so to speak, give the devil his due—in this case, meaning due acknowledgment of what he can do in regard to moving or *tempting us* toward sin. St. Thomas notes that the devil does not have power over our free will. Scripture tells us, for example: "Resist the devil and he will fly from you" (James 4:7). The devil can tempt us by stirring our sensitive appetites and imaginations, feeding us with impulses and images that lure us toward sin, but God has not allowed him dominion over our intellectual souls. As Augustine noted, "Nothing else than his own will makes man's mind the slave of his desire."[75] How important it is, then, to train ourselves in virtue and to render ourselves open to God's grace, so that we may more easily "Just say no!" to the devil.

The buck stops with us

External causes, things outside of us, can act only as inducements or partial causes of sins. Things, people, or events may stir our senses or work to sway our reason toward thoughts and acts of covetousness, gluttony, lust, hate, or a variety of other sins, but they are not sufficient causes of sin in and of themselves. To sin, we must consent with our wills. "The buck stops here for sin," we might say—and "here" is in our own hearts.

Internal causes of sin include *ignorance*. If someone is truly ignorant of the sinful nature of an act, it may excuse the guilt of a sin, since he did not know the act was morally wrong. This reduces the voluntariness (willfulness) of the wrong, but

[74] *ST*, I-II, Q. 80, art. 3.
[75] Ibid., art. 1.

ignorance is no excuse for sin when it pertains to things we have an obligation to know. Some people may purposely remain ignorant in order to sin more freely. "Wherefore all are bound in common to know the articles of the faith, and the universal principles of right, and each individual is bound to know matters regarding his duty or state."[76] *Passion* is another internal cause of sin. For example, when our sense appetites are stirred toward such powerful emotions as anger, we may succumb to a rage in which we do things contrary to reason. In extreme cases, powerful emotions that precede sins may temporarily override reason, render one temporarily insane, and reduce the moral culpability for sin. We must all try to control our passions with reason, nonetheless, and we must especially avoid purposefully stirring our own wills to motivate ourselves toward sinful acts of passion — for example, dwelling on revenge. The worst of the internal causes of sin is *malice*, or ill will, which is a rational, cold, calculated, and willful choice of evil over good, unclouded by ignorance or the heat of passion.

Can *sin* cause sin?

St. Thomas noted in the quotation that begins this chapter that sin involves "forsaking the one for the many." When we sin, we forsake the ultimate goodness of God for the many lesser temporal goods we desire. God would have us love ourselves, but after, and not contrary to, our love of him and neighbor. When we sin, we declare that we love ourselves foremost. "Therefore it is evident that inordinate love of self is the cause of every sin."[77]

---

[76] *ST*, I-II, Q. 76, art. 2.
[77] *ST*, I-II, Q. 77, art. 4.

St. Paul tells us, "The desire of money is the root of all evils" (1 Tim. 6:10). As roots provide the nourishment that a noxious vine needs to thrive and grow, so does covetousness seek riches that can provide means for someone to satisfy his desire for other sins. This is not to say that covetousness is the *only* root of evils, since other sins, such as ambition or gluttony, might lead a man toward *avarice* (another name for covetousness) for money. But other evils *more frequently* arise from the love of money.

We learn from Scripture that "the beginning of pride is sin" (Ecclus. 10:13). Thomas notes that *pride* in the sense of *an inordinate desire to excel* is the beginning of sins, including covetousness, in the sense that "man's end in acquiring all temporal goods is that, through their means, he may have some perfection and excellence. Therefore, from this point of view, pride, which is the desire to excel, is said to be the beginning of sin."[78] But from a practical point of view, so to speak, "the first place belongs to that by which, furnishing the opportunity of fulfilling all desires of sin, has the character of a root, and such are riches; so that, from this point of view, covetousness is said to be the *root* of all evils."[79]

What are the seven deadly "captains" of sin?

We saw that sins such as pride and avarice can lead to other sins. These sins and five others are known as *capital* sins. St. Thomas points out that the word *capital* comes from the Latin word *caput*, meaning "head." When we speak of capital sins, we are using the word *capital* in the metaphorical sense, as in the "head" of a company or a state. Thomas notes that St. Gregory

[78] *ST*, I-II, Q. 84, art. 2.
[79] Ibid.

the Great compared the capital sins to the leaders of an army (perhaps like *captains*). In this case, the soldiers are a multitudinous variety of sins and misdeeds; the capital sins are the officers who set them to their nefarious tasks. These seven capital (also known as "deadly") sins are: pride, avarice, envy, wrath, lust, gluttony, and sloth.

The capital sins "engender other sins, other vices."[80] The ancient Church Fathers called the sins they spawned the "daughters" of the capital sins. For example, St. Thomas approved of St. Gregory's list, which identified "hatred, tale-bearing, detraction, joy at our neighbor's misfortunes, and grief for his property" as daughters of *envy*. The daughters of *avarice* are treachery, fraud, falsehood, perjury, restlessness, violence, and insensitivity to mercy. We need only turn on the news any day to see the daughters of covetousness at play on the personal, national, and international levels. But some sins are much more serious than others, and it is time to look at the most crucial distinction.

Danger and damnation

The word *mortal* used for grave sin comes from the Latin *mors* ("death"), while the word *venial* used for less serious sins comes from *venia* ("pardon"). Mortal sin destroys infused charity in our hearts, stains our souls, and leads to spiritual death and, if we remain unrepentant, to eternal damnation. In mortal sin we deliberately turn away from God. Our *Catechism* (no. 1857) explains that for a sin to be considered mortal, three things are required: "Mortal sin is sin whose object is grave matter and which is also committed with full knowledge and deliberate consent."[81]

---

[80] *Catechism of the Catholic Church*, no. 1866.
[81] *ST*, I-II, Q. 83, art. 2.

Venial sins are small moral transgressions that warrant a limited, temporal punishment either on earth or in the fires of purgatory. St. Paul likens venial sins to "wood, hay, stubble," that can be tested and burned with fire, so that while a "man's work is burned up, he will suffer loss, though he himself will be saved, but only as through fire" (1 Cor. 3:12, 15, RSV). Venial sins cause disorder in our souls, but do not destroy them, though they may plant the seeds and help establish vicious habits under which mortal sins can take root.

What of the one and only Original Sin?

Adam and Eve, the first parents of humanity, committed the original, personal sin, in which they essentially chose their own desires over those of God. This "sin of nature" produced a fallen human nature, which all of us ever since (except Jesus and Holy Mother Mary) have inherited through our common humanity. Original Sin affects our souls primarily through the disordering of our wills. It is because of Original Sin that we suffer from *concupiscence*, the inclination to sin, which we can resist through our wills and by the grace of Christ.

CHAPTER NINE

Law: A Guide toward a Goal

The light of natural reason, whereby we discern what is good and what is evil, which is the function of the natural law, is nothing else than the rational creature's participation of the eternal law.

—ST, I-II, Q. 91, art. 2

After addressing sin, St. Thomas declares it is time to consider the "extrinsic principles of acts."[82] The principle outside of us inclining us toward evil is the devil.[83] The extrinsic principle inclining us toward good is almighty God himself, and he does so by means of *instruction* through his *law* and the *assistance* of his *grace*. God's lawful instruction and graceful assistance are the matter of our next two chapters.

While the foundation of St. Thomas's approach to the moral life of man is development of virtue, the various kinds of law work hand-in-hand with virtue, since the ultimate goal of both is human happiness. St. Isidore of Seville wrote that "laws are enacted for no private profit, but for the common benefit

---

[82] *ST*, I-II, Q. 90, prologue.
[83] *ST*, I, Q. 114; I-II, Q. 80.

of citizens," and Aristotle explained that just laws "are adapted to produce and preserve happiness and its parts for the body politic."[84] Thomas adds, "The last end of human life is bliss or happiness . . . Consequently, the law must needs regard principally the relationship to happiness."[85]

Laws, then, act as "extrinsic principles"—commands from outside of us that prompt us to act justly and virtuously, so as to maximize our own happiness and that of our neighbor.

What is eternal law?

Lex ("law") comes from the Latin word *ligare* ("to bind") because laws bind us to act in certain ways, commanding us to do some things and forbidding us from doing others. Within each person, our *reason* plays the commanding role. Within the universe as a whole, the *divine reason* of God is the supreme commander. The ultimate law from which all other varieties exist, move, and have their being is the *eternal law* of God, for Thomas notes that "the eternal law is nothing else than the type of Divine Wisdom, as directing all actions and movements."[86] Eternal law reflects the divine providence through which God foresees, orders, and governs all things. In a real, but incomplete sense, the eternal law is imprinted in every human heart. While only the blessed who see God in his essence can understand the eternal law directly, everyone knows it "in its reflection, greater or less. For every knowledge of truth is a kind of reflection and participation of the eternal law, which is the unchangeable truth, as Augustine says (*De Vera. Relig.* xxxi)."[87]

---

[84] *ST*, I-II, Q. 90, art. 2.
[85] Ibid.
[86] *ST*, I-II, Q. 93, art. 1.
[87] Ibid., art. 2.

What is natural law?

Of all God's creatures, we are subject to divine providence "in the most excellent way," because we can share in that providence by sharing in the governance of ourselves and other creatures: "The participation of the eternal law in the rational creature is called the natural law."[88] This is accomplished through the light of our natural reason, whereby we can determine good and evil, right and wrong, and discern our duties and obligations in accord with the fundamental principle — which is to do good and avoid evil.

What is the role of human law?

In producing *human laws*, we employ our practical reasoning to apply the general, fundamental principles of natural law to particular matters and acts. So then, courtesy of our God-given intellectual souls, we can come to know right and wrong and to promulgate laws, with the object of promoting what is right and good, for the benefit of all. If particular human laws are unjust, says St. Thomas, they do not bind us in conscience. This point was cited by Baptist minister Martin Luther King Jr. when opposing segregation laws. Writing from his Birmingham jail cell in August of 1963, King wrote: "To put it in the terms of St. Thomas Aquinas, an unjust law is a human law that is not rooted in eternal and natural law."

Thomas notes that one of the ways laws may be unjust is "when burdens are imposed unequally on the community . . . These are acts of violence, rather than laws."[89] Thomas recalls too, in this context, the words of Peter and the apostles, "We

---

[88] *ST*, I-II, Q. 91, art. 2.
[89] *ST*, I-II, Q. 96, art. 4.

must obey God rather than men" (Acts 5:29, RSV). Since human laws are made by fallible men, they must be subject to change if they are unjust.

Due to the limitations of natural reason, it was necessary for God himself to *reveal* to us his divine, eternal law for four key reasons:

1. Laws guide men toward their proper ends, and our ultimate end is not natural, earthly happiness, but heavenly eternal happiness, which exceeds the grasp of natural reason and requires a law given directly by God.

2. Human judgments may differ, but a law given directly by God is certainly without error.

3. Only God is competent to make laws about people's interior actions, such as thoughts and desires.

4. Human law cannot punish every evil without doing away with much good, but God's law can forbid all sins.

What was the Old Law?

God's divine law was first revealed through the "Old Law" preserved in the Old Testament. This was a good, but imperfect or incomplete law, designed to repress sinful passions and acts and to prepare the way for the perfect law of charity that Christ would later bring. The old law was "given by God through the angels,"[90] and consisted of *moral precepts* to build virtue in man and to "establish man in friendship with God,"[91] *ceremonial precepts* to guide divine worship, and *judicial precepts* to provide

[90] *ST,* I-II, Q. 98, art. 1; citing Acts 7:53 and Gal. 3:19.
[91] *ST,* I-II, Q. 99, art. 2.

practical guides to regulate just conduct among God's Chosen People. While the ceremonial and judicial precepts of the Old Law were given specifically to the Jews, the moral precepts of the Old Law expressed the precepts of *natural law* and were (and still are!) binding on everyone. They are summed up in the Decalogue — the Ten Commandments given to Moses.

What's different about the New Law?

The "New Law" is the Law of the Gospel and of the New Testament, a perfect law of charity: "chiefly the grace itself of the Holy Ghost, which is given to those who believe in Christ."[92] The New Law is contained *virtually* in the Old Law as a tree is contained virtually in the seed from which it grows. The New Law guides us to eternal life with God. It *teaches* us about the faith to lead us to justification; and it *justifies* us, liberating us from sin through the action of "the grace of the Holy Spirit bestowed inwardly."[93] The New Law informs our interior lives and external actions, and is summarized in Christ's Sermon on the Mount. The external instruments of grace are the Seven Sacraments, and grace is rightly used by acts of charity.

[92] *ST*, I-II, Q. 106, art. 1.
[93] Ibid., art. 2.

CHAPTER TEN

Caught by Grace

*We must now consider the exterior principle of
human acts, i.e., God, in so far as, through grace, we
are helped by Him to do right; and first we must consider
the grace of God; secondly, its cause; thirdly, its effects.*

—*ST*, I-II, Q. 109, prologue

Can we achieve everlasting happiness without God's grace?

Nope. We cannot pull ourselves up to heaven by our own boot-
straps, no matter how long or how sturdy they may be! The
idea that we could fulfill God's commandments and merit eternal happiness through the proper use of our own free will and
natural powers was at the heart of the fifth-century Pelagian
heresy. Pelagius denied the Fall and Original Sin, and his errors
were refuted soundly by his contemporary St. Augustine. St.
Thomas tells us that despite our capacities to acquire natural
virtue, the attainment of eternal bliss with God is a *supernatural*
end, above any natural capacity, especially in our fallen state,
with our disordered appetites and wills.

But God comes gladly to our rescue with his freely given
sanctifying grace. This grace is a gift from God that not only
perfects the various *powers* of the soul as the *virtues* do but also

permeates and transforms the very *essence* of the human soul, from which the powers flow. Even the God-infused supernatural virtues of faith, hope, and charity flow from grace, their supernatural source. "For as the acquired virtues enable a man to walk in accordance with the natural light of reason, so do the infused virtues enable a man to walk as befits the light of grace."[94] If we're going to walk the walk of God, we need the light of his amazing grace.

What are the six varieties of grace?

Sanctifying grace: Grace given by God to a person to make him holy and to unite him to God as a participant in the divine nature.

Gratuitous grace: Grace given by God to a person to enable him to help lead *others* toward union with God.[95]

Operating grace: Grace that *directly moves us* to will and act, in which our minds are moved, but do not move (as when God gives us the grace to will good instead of evil).

Cooperating grace: Grace that *strengthens our will* and *gives us the capacities* to do "meritorious works, which

---

[94] *ST*, I-II, Q. 119, art. 3.

[95] Thomas further notes in *ST*, I-II, Q. 111, art. 4 that "the Apostle" (St. Paul) rightly further "divides" the gratuitous graces into wisdom, knowledge, miracles, prophecy, discerning of spirits, tongues, and interpretation of speeches (1 Cor. 12:8–10). By use of these special graces, their receivers display speech and deeds that God alone could produce, thereby teaching and persuading their hearers and witnesses to turn their hearts to God.

spring from the free-will," thus making us ready to receive operating grace and to put it to good use.[96]

Prevenient grace: Grace that *precedes* and *causes* a state or act of the soul.

Subsequent grace: Grace that *follows* as an *effect* of a prior effect of grace.[97]

What causes grace?

Grace is caused by a *who*—God alone. The gift of grace surpasses the power of any created nature, even that of the angels, "since it is nothing short of a partaking of the Divine Nature, which exceeds every other nature."[98] And get a load of just how amazing this grace really is: Thomas says that through grace "God alone should deify, bestowing a partaking of the Divine Nature by a participated likeness."[99] Through his grace, God,

---

[96] Thomas notes in *ST*, I-II, Q. 111, art. 3, however, that "operating and co-operating grace are the same grace; but are distinguished by their effects," that is, upon the intellect and will directly, or upon the operation of our free will. Both effects, of course, derive ultimately from God.

[97] This isn't going to make sense unless I lay it out the way Thomas did. He lists five effects of grace: 1) it heals the soul; 2) it helps us desire the good; 3) it helps us carry out acts to attain the good; 4) it helps us persevere in striving for the good; and 5) it helps our souls reach glory with God. Each of these effects acts as a cause (prevenient grace) to the effect (subsequent grace) that follows. Thomas notes too, in *ST*, I-II, Q. 11, art. 4, that "although the effects of grace may be infinite in number, even as human acts are infinite, nevertheless . . . all coincide in this—that one precedes another."

[98] *ST*, I-II, Q. 112, art. 1.

[99] Ibid.

in a sense, *deifies us* and makes us like him in a limited sense. We need to do our part to prepare our hearts for God's grace by turning our free will toward him. And yet even there, God alone is ultimately the cause and mover even of our free will. Grace, then, is truly and wholly a wondrous gift from God.

What is God's greatest work?

God's grace has two main effects: "1) the justification of the ungodly, which is the effect of operating grace; and 2) merit, which is the effect of co-operating grace."[100] Justification is the remission of our sins through the infusion of grace in our souls. The justification of ungodly sinners requires two acts of the free will: "one, whereby it turns to God's justice; the other whereby it hates sin."[101] And here's something you don't hear every day: *The justification of sinners is the greatest of all the wondrous works of God.* Although the creation of the universe is immeasurably greater in magnitude, it ends in the changeable good of nature, while the good of grace in even one soul ends "at the eternal good of a share in the Godhead."[102]

Can we merit our heavenly reward?

In a sense, yes we can! "It is written (Jer. 31:16): *There is a reward for thy work.* Now a reward means something bestowed by a reason of merit. Hence it would seem that a man may merit from God."[103] We cannot lay claim as a *right* to anything from God, since we are in no way his equal, and *all* of man's natural good comes from Him in the first place. God, nonetheless, has

---

[100] *ST*, I-II, Q. 113, prologue.
[101] Ibid., art. 3.
[102] *ST*, I-II, Q. 133, art. 9.
[103] *ST*, I-II, Q. 114, art. 2.

helped us achieve the merit that we could not achieve on our own. As a modern commentator on the *Summa* aptly explains, "the basis of this blessed situation lies in the fact that human free will, although moved by unmerited grace, actually does cooperate with God's will in accepting and using grace."[104] So then, we can *merit* even our heavenly reward, but only with the help of God's *grace*.

If we should turn away from God after receiving his grace and fall into mortal sin, we cannot merit for ourselves a restoration to grace after our fall; our restoration must be a work of God's grace. When in a state of grace, we may, however, merit an increase of grace or charity. Thomas cites Proverbs 4:18: "But the path of the just as a shining light, goeth forward and increaseth even to perfect day, which is the day of glory."[105] Thomas notes that every meritorious act causes an increase of grace, and the last end of grace is eternal life. "But just as eternal life is not given at once, but in its own time, so neither is grace increased at once, but in its own time, viz., when a man is sufficiently disposed for the increase of grace."[106]

If *The One-Minute Aquinas* is doing its job, *you* should be getting *fired up* for an increase in grace and charity. Let's move along now so St. Thomas can show us how to turn up that heat.

[104] Msgr. Paul J. Glenn, *A Tour of the Summa* (Rockford, IL: TAN Books, 1978), 183.
[105] ST, I-II, Q. 114, art. 8.
[106] Ibid.

69

DUMB OX BOX #3
Is it a sin to be curious?

Perhaps you've heard the saying "Curiosity killed the cat," and maybe its rejoinder, "but satisfaction brought him back." How curious it is that the learned saint who would not have us be boring or hate wine does warn us not to be curious. This may seem sour medicine in our enlightened times when "inquiring minds want to know." Well, let's read the Angelic Doctor's own prescription: "Studiousness is directly, not about knowledge itself, but about the desire and study in pursuit of knowledge . . . On the other hand, the desire or study in pursuing knowledge of truth may be right or wrong" (ST, II-II, Q. 167, art. 2).

Thomas considers the *vice of curiosity* as opposed to the *virtue of studiousness*, not in the context of the intellectual virtues, but in the context of the moral virtue of *temperance*. Curiosity derives from the word *cura* ("care"), and "man's mind is drawn, on account of his affections, toward the things for which he has an affection, according to Matt. 5:21, *Where thy treasure is, there is thy heart also*" (ST, II-II, Q. 166, art. 1).

Curiosity, then, is a wrongful desire or study in pursuing knowledge that violates the temperance that moderates our desires for things. We are curious when we focus our minds on knowledge that is sinful or trivial, rather than on true wisdom, when we seek knowledge for our own pride, rather than God's glory, and when we seek knowledge of the bizarre and the lurid, rather than of the true and the beautiful.

Our own age tempts us toward curiosity as never before, since a virtual universe of triviality is but a tap of a finger or a mouse click away. We'd be well advised, then, to follow the advice and the example of studious St. Thomas and focus our desires and studies on the matters that matter the most!

CHAPTER ELEVEN

Faith: The Foundation of Reason

For when a man's will is ready to believe, he loves the truth he believes, he thinks out and takes to heart whatever reasons he can find in support thereof; and in this way human reason does not exclude the merit of faith but is a sign of greater merit.

—*ST*, II-II, Q. 2, art. 10

Who needs faith in our scientific age?

We all need faith today as never before. Faith is under attack by many influential scientific (in many cases, merely "scientific"[107]) thinkers. Best-selling atheist biologist Richard Dawkins, for example, has defined faith as "belief without evidence," and has written concerning the faithful, "Virtuoso believers who can manage to believe something really weird, unsupported and unsupportable, in the teeth of the evidence and reason, are es-

---

[107] Deriving from "scientism": the belief that the methods of science are capable of addressing all the important questions about reality. (Ironically, the belief itself is philosophical and cannot be verified by the methods of science.)

pecially highly regarded."[108] Many voices cry out from today's secular wilderness that faith is a childish and primitive mode of thought, something for the naive, the dimwitted, and even the delusional. They deny any kind of supernatural reality and see *reason* (as perfected by naturalistic science) and faith as polar opposites and mortal enemies.

Ridiculous. Haven't they read the Second Part of the Second Part of the *Summa Theologica*?[109]

Philosopher Josef Pieper notes that in the dramatic climax of Homer's *Odyssey*, Odysseus throws off his disguise, is magnified in stature by the goddess Athena, bends the bow none of his enemies could bend, and slays his faithful wife's suitors. It was Thomas, Pieper says, to whom God gave the power to bend the mighty bow of truth, with faith and reason as its limbs, loosing its arrows like no other man. It's time now to take up that bow to see if Thomas can help *us* hit the mark.

What is faith?

St. Paul tells us that "faith is the substance of things to be hoped for, the evidence of things that appear not" (Heb. 11:1). Faith, then, implies a certainty (assurance) and belief (conviction) of the things that we are unable to see with our eyes, or detect with any of our senses, in our earthly state. What is it that we hope for? Eternal life. What is it that we cannot see? God himself, primarily. And what is the object of certain belief? The ultimate truth, which is God. Faith is *not* a belief

---

[108] Richard Dawkins, *The God Delusion* (New York: Mariner Books, 2008), 232.

[109] Readers are directed to a masterful, modern presentation and refutation of these modern views as well in Bl. Pope John Paul II's 1978 encyclical *Fides et Ratio* ("Faith and Reason").

in things *contrary* to the evidence of our senses or the logical rules of our reason, but is belief in things *beyond* them that God has revealed to man. Indeed, when we are in heaven with God, faith will no longer be needed, because the unseen will then be seen.

Thomas tells us that the virtue of faith resides primarily in the *intellect*, because its object is *truth*. In that way it bears relation to the *natural*, intellectual virtues of science, understanding, and reason, but faith operates on a higher *supernatural* plane, being one of the three theological virtues (along with hope and charity) that flow from God's grace and are infused in our souls. Fr. Réginald Garrigou-Lagrange has observed: "Faith may be likened to the sun, and science or knowledge to a candle, but nothing need prevent the sun and a candle from shedding light on the same object together."[110] The ultimate object of faith is God, but through his actions he has revealed many other things that we know as the articles of the Catholic faith. These range from the fundamental articles of faith in the Trinity and the Incarnation to many other truths articulated in our creeds and doctrines—as the Church is guided toward greater understanding of the faith over the centuries. Faith also involves the operation of the will when our free will, under the influence of God's grace, moves our intellects to assent to and believe in the things of God.

What is faith good for?

In referring to Hebrews 11:1, cited above, Thomas writes, "If anyone would reduce the foregoing words to a definition, he

---

[110] R. Garrigou-Lagrange, *The Theological Virtues*, vol. 1, *On Faith* (St. Louis: B. Herder Books, 1965), 114.

may say that *faith is a habit of the mind, whereby eternal life is begun in us, making the intellect assent to what is non-apparent.*"[111] Note well the phrase "whereby eternal life is begun in us." Thomas reminds us, "Without faith it is impossible to please God."[112] Even though our reason may convince us of God's existence,[113] we cannot attain salvation and eternal life unless we have faith and believe in what God has revealed to us as well. So then, faith is good for opening the door that leads to our heart's ultimate desire — eternal happiness with God, and in some sense, it begins as soon as we have faith and accept God's grace in our heart.

Thomas notes two main effects of faith as well. Although this might seem odd at first glance, faith produces *fear*. "It is written (James 2:19): *The devils . . . believe and tremble.*" Whether a man or a fallen angel believes in the existence of God's law, it can produce a selfish fear of punishment should one transgress his eternal law. This is called *servile fear* and reflects a *lifeless faith.* But faith brought to life by the supernatural virtue of charity, produces *filial fear,* a fear of doing wrong, lest one let God down and be separated from him. The second, clearly positive effect, declared by Peter in Acts 15:9, is that *faith cleanses* or *purifies the heart.*[114] Thomas says our hearts become impure when we love transient, created things in themselves, and they become purified by loving God, who is above all things. Faith begins that process of purification by turning our minds toward God. Charity completes it by perfecting our will to love all created things through God and to love God above all things.

[111] *ST*, II-II, Q. 4, art. 1.
[112] *ST*, II-II, Q. 2, art. 3.
[113] Stay tuned for chapter 22 for that!
[114] *ST*, II-II, Q. 7, art. 2.

How can we build faith in our souls?

The virtue of faith, unlike the natural virtues, is infused in our souls, so we must bear in mind that its foundation is built in us by the grace of God. But are there things *we* can do to grow in our faith? Absolutely! For starters, let's recall St. Thomas's quotation from the start of this chapter. Contrary to those who hold faith and reason in opposition, Thomas exclaims that when we love the truth God had revealed to us, we can use our God-given reason to support it — to understand it and defend it. It's one of the very reasons Thomas assembled the *Summa Theologica* and why we put together *The One-Minute Aquinas!* We can grow in faith by reception of the sacraments and by prayerful immersion in Scripture and in the teachings of the Church.

Even as we strive to increase in the virtue of faith, God provides further aid; for instance, in sending us the gifts of the Holy Spirit, which flow from faith. Through the *gift of understanding*, our natural capacity to "penetrate into the heart of things" penetrates even further and into the higher things of God. We come to understand better the articles of the faith and principles to guide our personal behavior, not only according to the light of human reason, but *according to the supernatural light of the guidance of the Holy Spirit.* Understanding gives us "a sound grasp of the things that are proposed to be believed," while the *gift of knowledge* gives us "a firm and right judgment on them so that we can discern what is to be believed from what is not to be believed."[115] In simple English, understanding says, "Yes, I get what you are saying," whereas knowledge says, "And I see that it is true [or false]."

[115] *ST*, II-II, Q. 9, art. 1.

The Catholic faith, then, is not opposed to reason and is not for dummies. Take the leap of faith, and you'll come to know and understand it.

CHAPTER TWELVE

Hope: The Courage to See the Truth

*The proper and principal object
of hope is eternal happiness.*

—*ST*, II-II, Q. 17, art. 2

The supernatural hope infused in our soul through God's grace is a virtue that seeks eternal happiness in union with God, which is "a future good, difficult but possible to obtain."[116] Virtues make us good and make our deeds good too. Something is possible to us if we can achieve it through our own efforts or through help from others. "Wherefore," Thomas says, "in so far as we hope for anything as being possible to us by means of the Divine assistance, our hope attains God himself, on Whose help it leans. It is therefore evident that hope is a virtue since it causes a human act to be good and to attain its due rule."[117]

While the *object* of hope is eternal bliss with God, the *subject* of hope (i.e., where it resides in our souls) is in the *will*. After the light of faith opens the eyes of our *intellect* to *see* and *believe* in the *truth* of God, our *wills* are drawn by hope to *seek* the

---

[116] *ST*, II-II, Q. 17, art. 1.
[117] Ibid.

goodness that comes from union with God, and also to *trust* in God that *he will help us* to attain eternal happiness with him.

Josef Pieper said hope captures "the very foundation of being in the world for the Christian: the concept of the *status viatoris.*"[118] A *viator* is "one on the way," and is translated as "wayfarer" in the *Summa Theologica*. Through the virtue of hope, we recognize that our very being depends on God, and the state of our eternal soul depends on our relationship with God during our brief stay on earth. With hope we know where we want to go and trust God to guide us there.

What is hope good for?

Hope is a God-given aid that can help us attain eternal life, but no virtue exists in a vacuum. As there can be a lifeless faith without charity ("for even as the body without the spirit is dead; so also faith without works is dead" [James 2:26]), there likewise can be a lifeless hope that merely seeks God *as a source of good for ourselves.* When charity provides the "spirit" to the "body" of hope, it is "quickened" or brought to life and we seek God *for his own sake.* Hence the truth of the terse summation "faith sees, hope seeks, and charity loves." (Thank God that he so freely gives us all three, if we are willing to receive them!) When our hope is livened by charity, we hope for the eternal bliss, not just of ourselves, but of others, even for our enemies.

A living hope will also help us grow in the twin virtues of *magnanimity* and *humility*, while we avoid the twin sins of *despair* and *presumption*. Recall that the aim of hope is a "difficult" good. We cannot climb to heaven on ladders of our own

[118] Josef Pieper, *Faith, Hope, Love* (San Francisco: Ignatius Press, 1977), 91.

making. *Magnanimity* is the "greatness of soul" through which we are confident we can achieve difficult goods. *Humility* is not its opposite, but its partner in truth and deed—whereby we remember that we can achieve great and difficult things *with God's help*. In St. Paul's words, "I can do all these things in him who strengthen me." (Phil. 4:13).

Deficiency in the virtue of hope can become the sin of *despair*, in which we give up hope of heaven, believing there is no chance for us—thus denying God's power and rejecting his mercy. Inflated, distorted hope can lead us to the sin of *presumption*, in which we assume our salvation is assured with no necessary effort on our part; we are thus in our minds magnifying our own power and rejecting God's justice. Despair arises from spiritual *sloth*, in which we value earthly goods and pleasures more than spiritual goods, while *presumption* arises from vainglory—in modern language, a narcissistic sense of entitlement. In many ways, our popular culture reveals that ours is an age of rampant despair *and* presumption. But with God, there is always hope!

How can we grow more hopeful?

Hope is expressed in the very act of petitionary prayer, in which we ask God for good things and express our trust that he will provide them. St. Thomas wrote, "Prayer is recommended to men, that by it they may obtain from God what they hope to secure from Him."[119] Indeed, his unfinished treatise on hope in his *Compendium of Theology* was to be built on an explication of the Lord's Prayer.

---

[119] *Aquinas's Shorter Summa* (Manchester, NH: Sophia Institute Press, 2002), 334.

As with all the theological and cardinal virtues, God has provided a special gift of the Holy Spirit to help us perfect the virtue of hope—the gift of *fear of the Lord* (Isa. 11:2). St. Thomas addresses a paradox here, since hope pertains to goods, and fear to evils. The fear of the Lord helps man to hope for the good by helping him *avoid the evil* that would deprive him of it. God, of course, is the ultimate good. Proper *fear* motivates us to avoid the evil of the just punishment that God may administer if we turn from his ways, and also of the privation we may suffer if we should come to a state of separation from him through our faults.

The flip side of the eternal law to "avoid the evil" is to "do the good." Hope directly seeks that good. As Thomas sums things up, "His justice gives rise to fear, but the consideration of His mercy gives rise to hope, so that, accordingly, God is the object of both hope and fear, but under different aspects."[120] The gift of fear serves as *the beginning of wisdom*, as we learn in Psalm 111:10,[121] and can lead us to the beatitude of *poverty of spirit*, says St. Thomas: "From the very fact that a man submits to God, it follows that he ceases to seek greatness either in himself or another, but only seeks it only in God."[122]

[120] *ST*, II-II, Q. 19, art. 1.
[121] Ibid., art. 7
[122] Ibid., art. 12.

CHAPTER THIRTEEN

Charity: To Love God through Our Neighbor

Charity is the friendship of man for God.

—ST, II-II, Q. 23, art. 1

Is love an actual virtue? You might tell me that "love is a passion of the concupiscible appetite whereby we experience a natural affinity for the good," leaving me little choice but to acknowledge your exemplary powers of memory concerning our chapter on the passions.

But here we speak of the love that is the theological virtue of *charity* that God infuses into the soul. Through faith we know God; through hope we desire to be with him and trust in him to help us do so; through charity we come to love God for his own sake and to love others and ourselves through our love in him. Charity resides not in our passions, but in the *will*, and the will desires, seeks, and loves the good. Love in the sense of charity seeks the highest good—the attainment of union with God.

St. Thomas begins his lengthy treatise on charity by showing how charity is really a state of *friendship* between man and God, citing 1 Corinthians 1:9: "*God is faithful; by Whom you are called unto the fellowship of His Son.* Love based on this friendship is charity; wherefore it is evident that charity is the friendship of man for God."

The love for what is good for ourselves is a love of concupiscence such as we might experience for a fine wine or a favorite horse (Thomas's own examples). In the love of *true* friendship, we love the friend for his own sake and not merely for the fact that he is useful or provides us with pleasure. We rejoice in our friend's existence, want to be with him, and wish the best for him and those dear to him. Not only do we wish him well—we take actions for his benefit to express that love. What an amazing honor that the Creator of the universe has extended his deepest friendship to each of us. Indeed, not only does God's friendship express his joy *that* we exist; it actually *causes* us to exist!

What's love got to do with it?

It is charity that makes faith and hope come alive. That's why St. Paul calls it the greatest of the three theological virtues (1 Cor. 13:13) and tells us that if he had the tongues to speak to angels, prophetic powers, understanding of mysteries, and enough faith to move mountains, but had not love, he would "be nothing" and "gain nothing." (1 Cor. 13:1–3). St. Thomas calls charity the mother of all the virtues, since "every virtue depends on it in a way."[123] As we shall see in the next chapter, all the *moral* virtues depend on prudence to determine the right means to put them into action, prudence being the practical wisdom that seeks virtuous means to attain virtuous ends. But how do we determine which *ends* are virtuous? Truly virtuous ends are those that derive from charity. When Jesus summed up

[123] *ST*, II-II, Q. 22, art. 1.

the law and the commandments by telling us to love God with all our hearts and our neighbors as ourselves, he commanded us to live the life of charity.

Thomas says that the "principal act of charity . . . is to love."[124] When we exercise the love of charity, it honors God, benefits our neighbor, and provides us with three main interior effects:

1. It brings spiritual *joy* when we participate in God's divine good. This joy will be perfect and eternal in heaven—indeed, the joy of the blessed will be "overfull, since they will obtain more than they were capable of desiring."[125]

2. It brings *peace* because peace is the calm tranquillity that comes internally when our desires are all directed to one object (the love of God) and between people when our desires are also all directed to the one object of God.

3. Charity results in *mercy* as well—a heartfelt sympathy for others' distress that will prompt us to take action to comfort them.

How hot is the furnace of *your* love?

St. Thomas compares the love of charity to the heat of a powerful furnace.[126] When our hearts burn with the fires of charity, their far-reaching flames serve to warm strangers and even our enemies. But since those closest to the furnace receive the most heat, true charity should begin at home, and be di-

[124] ST, II-II, Q. 27, prologue.
[125] ST, II–II, Q. 28, art. 3; cf. 1 Cor. 2:9.
[126] ST, II-II, Q. 27, art. 7.

rected in greatest intensity to the Spirit who dwells within our hearts, and to those who are near to us—our families, friends, school- or workmates, neighbors, and fellow parishioners. Thomas makes clear that we are indeed called to love *ourselves*, and even our *own bodies* with the love of charity. So how can we fan the flames of the charity God places within our hearts?

Although charity, as a theological virtue, is infused into our hearts by God, it can increase or decrease through our actions. St. Thomas tells us with moving eloquence how each act of charity increases within us the disposition or tendency to more charitable acts, "and this readiness increasing, breaks out into an act of more fervent love, and strives to advance in charity, and then this charity increases actually."[127] Aristotle says that we become builders by building and harpists by playing the harp. Thomas tells us we become fervent lovers by loving fervently!

One of my favorite Aquinas quotes: "The love of our neighbor requires that not only should we be our neighbor's well-wishers, but also his well-doers."[128] Charity is a dynamic virtue that acts and works and gets good things done—all through our love for God.

What loving act will *you* do for your neighbor when you next set this book aside?

---

[127] *ST*, II-II, Q. 24, art. 6.
[128] *ST*, II-II, Q. 32, art. 5; cf. 1 John 3:18.

CHAPTER FOURTEEN

Prudence Gets It Done

Prudence is right reason applied to action.

—*ST*, II-II, Q. 47, art. 8

Prudence holds a special place as both an intellectual and a moral virtue. On the "right reason" side of the definition, prudence is an *intellectual* virtue by which we *figure out the best action to take*. On the "applied to action" side, it is a *moral* virtue by which we figure out the best way *to get things done*. Prudence, then, is a *practical wisdom* that lives at the intersection of the true and the good, the intellect and the will, thought and action, the universal and the singular. Prudence seeks out the most effective and moral means for achieving virtuous ends, and it directs us in their execution. Do you want to do someone *justice*, set up a *temperate* diet that will keep your bodily temple healthy, develop the *fortitude* to study hard and diligently, or perhaps to heat up the *charity* burning in the furnace of your soul? It's prudence's job is to get the job done.

Did you know that virtues have "parts"?

St. Thomas says all virtues have "parts [that] are of three kinds, namely, *integral*—as wall, roof, and foundations are parts of a house; *subjective*—as ox and lions are parts of the animal kingdom; and *potential*—as the nutritive and sensitive powers are parts of the soul."[129] If you're prudent, you'll want to keep all three parts in stock. Next, we'll see how all of these parts comprise the house in our souls in which prudence dwells.

What are prudence's "gotta haves"?

Integral parts of the cardinal virtues are *other* virtuous habits that are necessary for the full expression of that cardinal virtue. They are the "gotta haves," which, as Thomas says, are like the walls and roof and foundation of a house.

There is always a future-looking component to prudence, hence its Latin name of *providentia*—"to see before," or to have foresight. When we select means to achieve our goals, we are making a prediction about what's going to work, but prudence is intermeshed with the present and the past as much as it is with the future. When we choose the means to attain our *future* goals, we act in the *present*, guided by what we have learned in the *past*. Before the birth of Christ, the Roman philosopher Cicero had defined the three parts of prudence as *memory, intelligence,* and *foresight*. St. Thomas's teacher St. Albert the Great, adopted them as well. Thomas combed the works of other philosophers too, including Aristotle and Macrobius, finally arriving at a list of *eight* parts.

Memory is the first integral part of prudence, because our practical decisions are guided by what we have learned in the past.[130] We need *understanding* to grasp how universal principles

---

[129] *ST*, II-II, Q. 48.

[130] *ST*, II-II, Q. 49, art. 1. St. Thomas even recommends a practice to improve the powers of one's memory in this article entitled "Whether Memory Is a Part of Prudence." Indeed, the method forms the core of my own two books on perfecting our

would apply in the concrete situations we face at the moment; *docility* (teachability) to enable us to acquire practical knowledge from others; *shrewdness* (the ability to think quickly) for situations in which we have no time to deliberate over our actions; *reasoning* to weigh the pros and cons of various possible courses of action when we *do* have time to deliberate; *foresight*, to anticipate accurately the possible results of our actions; *circumspection*, to consider all relevant circumstances; and *caution*, so that we do not rush in where angels fear to tread!

. . . and subjective parts?

Subjective parts of a virtue refer to the subject matter. For example, for the virtue of temperance, sobriety is the subjective part that regulates our passion for alcohol, and chastity is the subjective part that regulates our passion for procreation. So what about prudence? The subjective parts of prudence are the practical wisdom involved in *governing the self* and in *governing others*. We all bear the responsibility for guiding our own lives by our prudent actions, and some bear responsibility for governing some aspects of the lives of other people as well. Thomas describes four common forms of prudence needed for governing others as *reigning* prudence, needed by those who govern a people; *political* prudence that guides people in obeying government; *domestic* prudence involved in guiding a household, and *military* prudence displayed in the waging of war.[131] Surely, we pray that our leaders, fellow citizens, mothers, fathers, and generals will be prudent souls.

---

memories to store up Catholic truths: *Memorize the Faith!* and *Memorize the Reasons!*)
[131] *ST*, II-II, Q. 50, arts. 1–4.

Potential parts, also called secondary or annexed parts, describe related acts on matters that do not call forth the full
power of the virtue. The potential parts of prudence may all
sound Greek to you (because they are). Drawing here from Aristotle, Thomas lists *eubolia* (good counsel) as the potential virtue displayed when we seek wise counsel from others regarding
our possible courses of action. (It's related to *docility*.) *Synesis* is
the virtue of good judgment in particular matters that serve the
virtue of prudence. Lastly, *gnome* speaks not of little bearded
garden creatures, but of the ability to make wise practical judgments in extreme or unusual cases. (Perhaps King Solomon's
suggestion to cleave in twain the baby of disputing mothers is a
biblical example of *gnome* in action!)

How can we grow more prudent?

As with any natural virtue, we become what we think
about and do. One way to practice more prudent choices and
behaviors is to review the parts of prudence whenever you are
faced with a serious moral decision. Have you searched your
memory for relevant principles, sought to understand the situation in light of all possible circumstances and foreseeable out-
comes? If the situation does not admit of a quick and shrewd
judgment, have you sought out wise counsel and been willing
to learn from others, and even from relevant books and other
resources? Have you proceeded cautiously? And after you have
acted, will you observe the results and store them in the trea-
sury of memory to serve as a guide the next time a similar situation arises?

Thomas says, "It is proper to the rational creature to be
moved through the research of reason to perform any particular

action, and this research is called counsel."[132] But there is more to prudent counsel than natural reason. There is also a supernatural, infused prudence that God provides us when we are in a state of grace. The Holy Spirit also provides us with a gift that corresponds to prudence called "the spirit of counsel" (Isa. 11:2). Through the gift of counsel, our practical moral decisions are moved and guided not merely by reason, but by the stirrings of the Holy Spirit. When we say yes to God's gift of counsel and allow the infused habit of prudence to build within our souls, we will find moral means to godly ends. We avoid vices that counter prudence, such as foolish imprudence and slothful negligence, as well as impostor vices that mimic prudence—such as craftiness, cunning, and fraudulent acts that seek evil and deceptive means to attain evil ends.

[132] ST, II-II, Q. 52, art. 1.

DUMB OX BOX # 4

Is it fair to lay an ambush in war?

Perhaps you haven't asked yourself this question lately, but St. Thomas has the answer whenever you need it. He put it in his question 40, "Of War," in Part III of the *Summa*—in a discussion of the virtue of justice. This is yet another illustration of how thoroughly St. Thomas weighs the morality of all the actions of man.

Although Thomas cherishes the peace that flows from charity and wisdom, war was, and is, a reality, given man's fallen nature. Here, St. Thomas builds on the analysis of "just war" by St. Augustine (who himself had consulted St. Ambrose) to help determine what actions are ethical. For example, he notes that it is an offense against truth and justice to lie or break promises, even in the course of war—for example, by failing to honor a treaty or cease-fire, once one has committed to it—"for there are certain *rights of war and covenants, which ought to be observed even among enemies, as Ambrose states (On Duties, 1)*" (*ST*, II-II, Q. 40, art. 3).

But how about laying an ambush? That's okay. Thomas says there is nothing wrong in deceiving your enemy by *not revealing your plans or intentions.* He points out that, "even in the Sacred Doctrine, many things have to be concealed, especially for the nonbelievers, lest they deride it, according to Matthew 7:6—*Give not that which is holy to dogs.* Wherefore, much more ought the plan of campaign to be hidden from the enemy" (*ST*, II-II, Q. 40, art. 3).

Thomas cites an ancient manual on war, Frontinus's *Strategy*, and points out that to reject all deception as an affront to justice is unreasonable: "[A] man would have an inordinate will if he were unwilling that others should hide anything from him" (*ST*, II-II, Q. 40, art. 3).

CHAPTER FIFTEEN

Justice: Doing Right by God and Neighbor

Justice is a habit whereby a man renders to each one his due by a constant and perpetual will.

—*ST*, II-II, Q. 58, art. 1

On loan from God

God is just. We try to imitate him in our behavior toward him and toward each other. Thomas tells us the word *justice* derives from the Latin word *jus* (or *ius*), which means "right." What rights can our neighbors claim from us? Well, Americans know about "inalienable rights endowed in us by our Creator," and of "life, liberty, and the pursuit of happiness," to which our Founders refer in our Declaration of Independence. The concept of "inalienable rights" owes much to the theory of law—natural, manmade, and eternal—developed, as we saw in chapter 9, in the writings of St. Thomas.

Justice operates on two fundamental principles: its *integral parts* are "Do good!" and "Do no evil!" The justice of the law courts focuses primarily on the second, negative principle. We are not to deprive others of their rights to life, liberty, and the pursuit of happiness, or we must pay the penalty of the law.

There is also a positive side of justice, pronounced most fully by Christ himself when he gave us the summary of all the commandments: to love God with all our hearts and to love our neighbors as ourselves. For the follower of Christ, then, justice and charity are intertwined. We seek not only not to hurt our brother, but to help him. Christ's justice commands not merely that we *don't* do to others what we wouldn't want done to us, but that we proactively *do* unto others as we would have them do unto us.

Which virtues are annexed to the halls of justice?

We'll consider next, in rapid-fire succession, nine *potential*, *related*, or *annexed* virtues of justice on which Thomas spends about 170 pages of his more than 250-page treatise on justice (in double-column print) in the *Summa Theologica*. (Go there when you've more than a minute!)

Religion is a related "part" of the full virtue of justice; and as Thomas says, it's "the chief of the moral virtues."[133] If you recall, the first three of the Ten Commandments are directed toward giving God his due. But that brings up a puzzle and leads us to the reason religion is only a related part of justice: We owe God *everything*. So it's impossible for us to be strictly "just" to him—since the full definition of justice entails giving another his rightful due *in equal measure*. To put it mildly, that's beyond our ability. So our job is to give him our heartfelt devotion, like a small child making a gift for his parents—which, as parents know, can be of almost infinite value. St. Thomas goes on to describe the nature and proper exercise of *interior acts* of religion,

[133] *ST*, II-II, Q. 81, art. 6.

including devotion and prayer, and the *exterior acts* of religion, such as including adoration, sacrifice, oblations and firsfruits, tithes, oaths, and vows.

Piety is a related virtue in which we give *duty* (service) and *homage* (honor or reverence) to our parents and to our country, for "man is debtor chiefly to his parents and his country after God."[134]

Observance is a virtue by which we pay *dulia* (honor) and *obedience* to people who excel in some way, such as in possession of an office or role above us, such as a boss or an elected official. We should also note that, "in every man is to be found something that makes it possible to deem him better than ourselves."[135] *Everyone* is due some *dulia*!

Gratitude is a virtue by which we give thanks to God and to anyone who benefits us. The Roman philosopher Seneca wrote a whole book on it (*De Beneficiis*), and Thomas distills many guidelines to put this noble and beautiful virtue to practice. For instance: never discount a favor just because it was easy for the giver; never forget a favor; honor your benefactors by praising their deeds in conversations with others; and heal others' ingratitude toward us with additional beneficial acts—to give them more practice!

Vengeance speaks not of revenge or vigilantism, but is rather the habit of punishing wrongdoing within the realm of one's rightful authority—without cruelty, and in the spirit of helping the wrongdoers, or at least protecting their innocent victims.

Truth is a virtue that we owe to others. No one enjoys being lied to. We owe others the truth, as they owe the truth to us.

---

[134] *ST*, II-II, Q. 101, art. 2.
[135] *ST*, II-II, Q. 103, art. 2.

But there also are times that the virtue of truth bids us not to volunteer a harmful truth about another *unnecessarily*.

Friendliness or *affability* is also something we owe others, not in terms of a debt, but because we are social animals. St. Thomas calls it "a certain debt of equity, namely, that we behave pleasantly to those among whom we dwell."[136]

Liberality is that generosity with money that gives another not just what is rightly his, but what is rightly our own.

Epikea or *equity* is a virtue that applies in special cases: when true justice will be better served by *not* following the letter of an established human law.

How can we become more just?

Aristotle noted that "justice is a habit whereby a man renders to each one his due by a constant and perpetual will," and further, that "justice is a habit whereby a man is said to be capable of doing just actions in according with his choice."[137] Please note well the roles of habit, choice, will, and action. The capacity to be just to others must be built within ourselves through our habitual actions, day after day, by training our wills always to do what is right by our fellow man. Although it may not be easy, know that, according to Aristotle, "the most excellent of the virtues would seem to be justice, and more glorious than either the evening or the morning star."[138]

And what could be more glorious than all of the stars *and* all of the virtues? He who created them, of course. Thankfully, the Holy Spirit has also provided special help to us in a gift that

[136] *ST*, II-II, Q. 114, art. 2.
[137] *ST*, II-II, Q. 58, art. 1.
[138] *ST*, II-II, Q. 59, art. 12.

flows from the virtue of justice, when we are infused with God's grace. This is the *gift* of *piety*. Through the *virtue* of piety we honor our parents, and country, but through this *gift* of the Holy Spirit we pay worship to God *as Father*, which St. Thomas says "is yet more excellent than to pay worship to God as Creator and Lord."[139]

And there is more excellence yet. Through the gift of piety, we not only worship God as Father, but we honor all men because of their relationship to God the Father, as Thomas explains: "Hence it belongs to piety to honor the saints . . . and especially after the Day of Judgment, yet piety will exercise its principal act, which is to revere God with filial affection; for it is then above all that this act will be fulfilled, according to Wis. V. 5, *Behold how they are numbered among the children of God.* The saints will honor one another."

Don't you want to be in that pious number, when the saints go marching in?

---

[139] *ST*, II-II, Q. 121, art. 1.

CHAPTER SIXTEEN

Fortitude: Captain of the Soul

*Fortitude behaves well in
bearing all manner of adversity.*

—*ST*, II-II, Q. 123, art. 4

Got guts?

The virtue of *fortitude*, from the Latin *fortis* for "strength," speaks of something powerful deep within us. People of strong character are said to have "guts"—or humorously, "intestinal fortitude." A synonym for fortitude is courage, and *courage* derives from the Latin word *cor* for "heart." Aristotle called this virtue *andreia*, from the Greek for "manliness," implying valiance or bravery. Fortitude is not for the faint of heart. (Or perhaps it's just what they need.) It is sword and shield for the spiritual warrior we all (male and female) are called to be. It faces down the difficult to protect the good. Thomas tells us that fortitude is a virtue perfecting our irascible appetites that seek the arduous or difficult good by overcoming obstacles that get in our way. It is the guardian of the other virtues because "fortitude prevents the reason from being entirely overcome by bodily pain." Indeed, "the brave man has a stronger love for the good of virtue than for his own body."[140] This is seen in the acts of noble soldiers and of martyrs.

Fortitude concerns fear and daring. When we come under some form of attack, we may become fearful and withdrawn or enraged and aggressive, depending on the circumstances and our own temperament. The virtue of fortitude allows us to moderate our reaction appropriately; to overcome, as the case may be, undue fear or undue anger. It allows us to hit the golden mean between contrary vices of cowardice and recklessness.

Which two virtues make fortitude great?

In describing the "integral parts" of fortitude, St. Thomas describes two great positive virtues critical to the full expression of the virtue of fortitude.

Magnanimity derives from the Latin words *magnus* for "great" and *anima* for "soul." What a grand virtue is this "greatness of soul"! We are given great and powerful gifts from God, and we also have a fallen human nature, prone to sin. Magnanimity reflects our consideration of that divine spark within us, the recognition that we are greatly blessed by God and should use our powers for the greatest works of good within our capacities. While fortitude strengthens us to confront great and difficult evils, magnanimity strengthens us to obtain great and difficult goods. The magnanimous person's sights are set on high things, rather than "sweating the small stuff." Speaking of magnanimity, what great and difficult works for God's glory have *you* been focused on lately?

When you perform these works, you could wind up exercising *magnificence*. As you have probably surmised, magnificence

---

[140] *ST*, II-II, Q. 123, art. 8.

also derives from *magnus* ("great"). The *-ficence* half of the word is from the Latin *facere*, "to make or do." The virtue of magnificence is about *making* great things, principally through proper expenditure of money. Consider, for example, the enormous outlay of money and effort made by entire communities to erect the magnificent cathedrals and basilicas of Europe, some of which took more than a lifetime to build—so that those who began the work knew they would not live to see the finished product. Through fortitude we overcome undue fear of threats, and through magnificence we overcome fear of threats to our pocketbooks. We need to ask ourselves: Are there special projects associated with our church, or perhaps with the growth and support of Catholic media, where *we* might exercise the virtue of magnificence to help make something great for God?

Which two virtues make fortitude last?

Although magnanimity and magnificence stretch our minds toward the difficult goals of great deeds and acts, St. Thomas tells us that "the principal act of fortitude is to endure."[141] So now we turn to the two integral parts of fortitude that are all about enduring hard things.

Patience derives from the Latin *patientia*, and it is the ability to endure suffering. As a part of the virtue of fortitude, it describes our ability to endure suffering *without becoming sorrowful or defeated*. It also implies an ability to endure suffering produced from the outside, from the acts of another. Have you ever told someone, "You have the patience of a saint"? If so, chances are the saint-like one has endured with calmness and grace the annoying and bothersome behavior of another person—perhaps

[141] Ibid.

complaints, disrespect, or ingratitude from someone he was try-ing to help. Patience is essential to fortitude, since when we seek great goods, we must often bide our time. Many pleasures come quickly and easily, while virtuous rewards may be a long time in the making, sometimes a lifetime. It is patience that en-ables us to do the right things with gladness in our hearts, even while we endure present evils.

Perseverance is the second, defensive, enduring virtue essen-tial to fortitude. It enables us to endure to the end in committing virtuous acts, regardless of obstacles. To the magnificent man or woman, this might mean staying the course and providing whatever additional expenses are needed to fund a great pub-lic work beset with unexpected delays or costs. To the student, perseverance might mean continuing to study for an upcoming exam, even as social activities, TV, or social media threaten to distract us. And in the grandest sense, we must persevere in faith throughout our lives, for "he that shall persevere to the end, he shall be saved" (Matt. 24:13).

How do people miss the mark of fortitude?

Fortitude is a clear example of how virtues embody "golden means," of not too little and not too much. There are so many ways to miss the mark of fortitude by falling into vices of defi-ciency or excess related to fortitude or its integral parts. Thomas examines them in great depth, but we have just a minute, so please see the summary chart on the opposite page.

A gift to die for?

Pop quiz: What are the Seven Gifts of the Holy Spirit? Per-haps you recall from our chapter 7, drawing from Isaiah 11:2 that they are wisdom, understanding, counsel, fortitude (listed

The Golden Mean of Fortitude —
and the Fool's Gold of Its Counterfeits

Vices of Deficiency	Virtue or Part	Vices of Excess
Fearfulness or Cowardice	Fortitude	Foolhardiness Fearlessness Daring
Pusillanimity*	Magnanimity	Presumption Ambition Vainglory
Meanness or Stinginess	Magnificence	Waste
Impatience** Resignation	Patience	Subservience "Pseudo-martyrdom"
Effeminacy***	Perseverance	Obstinacy

---

 * "Smallness of soul" from the Latin word *pusillus*, meaning "very little," "petty," or "paltry." "Pusillanimity makes a man fall short of what is proportionate to his power . . . Hence it is that the servant who buried in the earth the money that he received from his master and did not trade with it through fainthearted fear, was punished by his master (*ST*, II-II, Q. 133, art. 1).

 ** St. Thomas did not detail the vices opposed to patience. I have suggested these vices of deficiency and excess based on the principles he applied to other virtues and vices. Interested readers with more than a minute at hand, see my *Unearthing Your Ten Talents*, pp. 89–91, for a detailed explication.

 *** *Effeminacy* does not imply that women cannot display perseverance, as lives of so many female saints attest. It means an inability to suffer hardship or toil due to an inappropriate love of pleasure, play, or leisure. It is a self-trained weakness and delicacy, a clear example of St. Thomas's dictum: "Virtue implies a perfection of power . . . Every evil is a weakness" (*ST*, I-II, Q. 55, art. 3).

as *might* in the Revised Standard Version of the Bible), knowledge, piety, and fear of the Lord. In case you didn't recall them, here's a chance to redeem yourself. Which of these gifts corresponds to the virtue of fortitude? Indeed, it's the *gift* of fortitude! The gift of fortitude accompanies some very serious matters. It has a special relationship to the sacrament of Confirmation. The bishop calls on the Holy Spirit to endow those newly confirmed with the spiritual gifts so that they might persevere in the life of faith. But how does the *gift* of fortitude differ from the *virtue* of fortitude?

The virtue of fortitude notes a "firmness of mind" both in doing good and in enduring evil, especially when those goods and evils are "arduous" or difficult. Still, it is not within our human powers to obtain every good and avoid every evil, and we may be overcome by death. So human fortitude cannot always obtain its ends. By the grace of the Holy Spirit, however, man ultimately can defeat even death by persevering in virtue and then enjoying eternal life, so that *through God's gift of fortitude, we can actually achieve our find end of the most arduous and highest good.* Further, through the gift of fortitude, a "certain confidence of this is infused into the mind by the Holy Ghost, Who expels any fear of the contrary."[142]

The ultimate act of fortitude is *martyrdom*.[143] Thankfully, few are called to the ultimate martyrdom at any one time. And yet, as the tenets of our faith come under increasing attack today by governmental bodies and popular culture in what some call the "post-Christian" era, we would all do well to build the virtue of fortitude within our souls and to cherish God's gift of fortitude, so that we may remain vigilant and persevere to the end.

[142] *ST*, II-II, Q. 139, art. 1.
[143] *ST*, II-II, Q. 124, art. 3.

CHAPTER SEVENTEEN

Temperance: Taming the Mind's Confusion

The end and rule of temperance
itself is happiness.

—*ST*, II-II, Q. 141, art. 6

What good is temperance?

The word *temperance* acquired a tarnished reputation in the twentieth century. The Temperance Movement achieved strict legal restrictions on the sale of alcohol, against which the public rebelled. Later in the century, "If it feels good, do it!" became the practical philosophy of a selfish culture that considered itself advanced and enlightened. If you argued for the virtue of temperance then, you had to be prepared to be labeled a prohibitionist, a Puritan, a Victorian, a repressed personality, or some other variety of sour-pussed party pooper!

Well, much of the "party" that was the second half of the twentieth century has pooped out on its own and brought with it all sorts of personal and social hangovers that continue to grow today. Freedom *from* temperance has brought all kinds of consequences, from increases in addictions, obesity, STDs, and divorce to that total eradication of a human being's freedom,

THE ONE-MINUTE AQUINAS

the deprivation—under color of human law—of the right to life and liberty through abortion.

St. Thomas knew about fallen human nature—which was the same in the thirteenth century as in the twenty-first—and he therefore knew how critical is the virtue of temperance. Its job is not at all to keep us from good things, but to keep us from fleeting, pleasant, *apparent* goods that will damage our souls and lead not to joy, but to disappointment and misery. Temperance's "end and rule" is happiness.

What does temperance flee?

Thomas tells us that "temperance withdraws man from things which seduce the appetite from obeying reason."[144] It is the virtue that moderates the concupiscible appetite, by which we desire things that *seem* good to us, specifically things that satisfy our senses through eating, drinking, and sexual behavior. In animals, these desires are guided virtually automatically by instinct, but in man, it is the job of reason to control them. If it doesn't, things like gluttony, addiction, drunkenness, obesity, and all the possible harmful consequences of unbridled sexual passion can follow.

Thomas tells us that the first integral part of the virtue of temperance is *shamefacedness*. Shame is what temperance flees. A temperate person will experience a shameful discomfort at the thought or reality of sinful, intemperate acts. Those lacking temperance will be shameless. Indeed, in some ways our modern popular culture has cast aside this integral part, granting celebrity and fame to many who most flaunt their own shamelessness. It's a shame to see how often celebrated, shameless

---

[144] *ST*, II-II, Q. 141, art. 2.

people who so influence others, themselves end in the abject unhappiness of addictions and self-destruction.

What does temperance seek?

Temperance seeks *honesty*. Honesty derives from the word for "honor," and honorable things possess true excellence. The temperate man is characterized by honesty in that his internal thoughts and his external acts and deeds are consistent. He will seek honesty as earnestly as he avoids shame, and it will provide order and beauty to his life. Plato said that if we were to see spiritual honesty with our eyes, it would "arouse a wondrous love of wisdom."[145]

Can we eat, drink, and be merry temperately?

Temperance is tasked with moderating or controlling the most powerful of our passions for all physical satisfactions. These, then, are the "subjects," the "subjective parts" of temperance.

Abstinence is the virtue that regulates with reason our desire for and consumption of food. It seeks the golden mean in consumption and helps us treat our bodies as temples of the Holy Spirit. It combats the vice of gluttony, which consists in an inappropriate desire for food in terms of eating too much, of wolfing down our food, of being too picky in our food choices, of just plain thinking about it too much, instead of more important things. Thomas summarizes the varieties of gluttonous behavior in the verse: "*Hastily, sumptuously, too much, greedily, daintily.*"[146]

Sobriety moderates our use of alcohol. This typically involves avoiding excessive drinking, although Thomas, in an intriguing

---

[145] *ST*, II-II, Q. 145, art. 2.
[146] *ST*, II-II, Q. 148, art. 5.

passage, notes that it is indeed possible to miss the target of the virtue of sobriety through an error of deficiency. How's that? Well, "if a man were knowingly to abstain from wine to the extent of molesting nature grievously, he would not be free of sin."[147] There are clearly some people with tendencies toward alcoholism who should not drink at all, but even those people should recognize that wine, beer, and the like are good things in themselves, despi e the fact that they must swear off them for their own personal reasons. "Hence it is written (Ecclus. xxxi. 37–38): *Sober drinking is health to the soul and body; wine drunken with excess raiseth quarrels, and wrath, and many ruins.*"[148] One should not drink to the point that it clouds reason, but to the point of a friendly lightheartedness and not beyond.

Which virtues are tasked with taming lust?

Thomas describes two "subjective parts" of temperance — *chastity* and *purity*, which deal with our most passionate desires for sexual relations. He notes that these desires are good in themselves and work toward the propagation of our species, but they are so powerful that they require strong virtues to keep them in line with reason, so they lead us to good instead of harm to ourselves and others. Before the Fall, this would have presented no problem, as man's intellect, will, and desires were aligned in a state of natural grace. Since that time, we've had a battle on our hands. St. Augustine tells us that "the most difficult combats are those of chastity; whereas the fight is a daily one, but victory rare." St. Isidore adds that the devil subjects mankind more by carnal lust than by anything else because "the

---

[147] *ST*, II-II, Q. 150, art. 1.
[148] Ibid.

vehemence of this passion is more difficult to overcome."[149] So how do we overcome it?

The virtue of chastity "*chastises* concupiscence, which, like a child, needs curbing, as the Philosopher states (*Ethic.* iii, 12)."[150] *Chastity* refers to restraint in sexual intercourse; *purity* restrains related sexual behaviors—such things as looks, thoughts, touch, and kisses. These virtues oppose the vice of lust, which treats others as objects of one's selfish sexual desires. An unfettered lust can be so engrossing that it gives birth to its "daughters" of "*blindness of mind, thoughtlessness, inconstancy, rashness, self-love, hatred of God, love of this world and abhorrence or despair of a future world.*"[151] So how can we build the charity and the purity to put lust in its place? Let's take a minute, and go again to Thomas.

Thomas's tip for keeping it real

Thomas provides one simple, deceptively abstract-sounding, yet exceedingly practical line that can be a big help: "Hence, the most effective remedy against intemperance is not to dwell on the consideration of singulars."[152] The pleasures brought through the sense of touch are the most powerful of all, especially those we derive from eating and from sex. Lust, the most powerful challenge to the virtue of temperance, thrives on singulars, especially for men on images of enticing bodies. Unfortunately, advertisers and the purveyors of popular media know this so well that we are under perpetual bombardment by seductive images designed to arouse our lusts. The styles of

[149] *ST*, II-II, Q. 154, art. 3.
[150] *ST*, II-II, Q. 151, art. 1.
[151] *ST*, II-II, Q. 153, art. 5.
[152] *ST*, II-II, Q. 142, art. 3.

The Cardinal Virtues and Their Parts

	Integral Parts	Subjective Parts	Potential Parts
Prudence	Memory Reason Understanding Shrewdness Docility Foresight Circumspection Caution	Governing self Governing others Reigning Political Domestic Military	Eubolia Synesis Gnome
Justice	Doing good Avoiding evil	Distributive Commutative	Religion Piety Observance Gratitude Vindication Truth Friendship Liberality Equity
Fortitude	Magnificence Magnanimity Patience Perseverance	*No separate parts: fortitude is about doing the arduous or difficult good.*	Constancy Confidence Strenuousness Manliness
Temperance	Shamefacedness Honesty	Abstinence Sobriety Chastity Purity	Continence Mildness Meekness Modesty Studiousness

dress, attitudes, and manners of behavior they promote bear fruit in the attire and demeanor of real flesh-and-blood men and women.

Males by their nature are greatly prone to distraction by these images, both through the media and in daily life. What does Thomas recommend? We should focus on the opposite of "singulars"—namely, "universals." Instead of turning the eyes and imagination to this or that particular woman, turn the mind to "woman." Focus on the woman's identity as a "daughter," or "sister," and perhaps as someone else's current or future "wife" or "mother."

The lustful man functions like an animal at the level of the sensitive soul. He perceives singular bodies and desires them, but does not strive to see the essence of the human souls within. He really loves only himself. Instead, men should emulate the man who shows true love for all women by honoring and respecting them. Married couples can treat each other with special loving attention as singulars, with the eyes of love, rather than lust.

How can we attain the beauty of a temperate character?

Thomas distinguishes the potential or connected virtue of *continence* from the perfected virtue of *temperance*. When you struggle mightily against that urge for a second gooey doughnut and choose not to have one, you have performed an act of *continence*. When you've trained your soul to the point that the second doughnut does not even tempt you (or not even the first!) then you have acted in *temperance*. Continence, though, can be a stepping-stone along the road to true temperance. The habitual practice of continence—saying no to our desires through repeated effortful acts—develops within us the virtue of temperance, which, when perfected, eliminates the internal struggle altogether.

When our characters are marked by a robust temperance, we will display as well the associated virtue of *meekness*, which regulates our anger—displaying it at the right time, toward the right person, for the right reasons, as Jesus did when cleansing the Temple. (Meekness is not weakness!) *Mildness* or *clemency* walks hand-in-hand with temperance too when we show restraint or leniency in inflicting a necessary punishment on those under our command (as perhaps, in the role of a boss or a parent). Whereas meekness regulates the passion of anger, mildness or clemency regulates its actions in external punishment. A fourth connected virtue is *modesty*, deriving from the word *mode*, or "the ordinary." Thomas advises that a modest person will dress in a manner fitting with the customs of one's society, and one's position or role, being neither ostentatious nor showing exaggerated plainness or simplicity (which may portray a spiritual pride[153]). *Studiousness* too, is a virtue connected to temperance. It tempers our desire for knowledge, so that we focus our attention on things that matter the most.

[153] *ST*, II-II, Q. 169, art. 1.

DUMB OX BOX #5
Is it a sin to belittle yourself?

Yes. So snap out of it! As Christians, we know we must be on guard against boastful pride, and arrogance. Yet even wise pagan philosophers have observed: *"It is the practice of boasters both to make overmuch of themselves, and to make very little of themselves*: and for the same reason it is related of Augustine that he was unwilling to possess clothes that were either too costly or too shabby, because by both do men seek glory" (*ST*, II-II, Q. 113, art. 2, citing Aristotle's *Nichomachean Ethics*, bk. 4, chap. 7 in the italicized section).

Thomas addressed this issue in his question on irony because the word *irony* derives from a Greek word meaning to speak falsely about one's own good points. We must be wary, then, of a false humility. We need not seek out ways to broadcast our talents to others, but neither should we deny that we have them or seek to hide them underneath bushel baskets. As Augustine has so aptly written, "If thou liest on account of humility, if thou wert not a sinner before lying, thou hast become one by lying" (cited in *ST*, II-II, Q. 113, art. 1).

CHAPTER EIGHTEEN

Graces: Extraordinary Powers from God

*After treating individually of all the virtues
and vices that pertain to men of all conditions
and estates, we must now consider those things
which pertain especially to certain men.*

—*ST*, II-II, Q. 171, prologue

Got graces to give?

We saw in chapter 10 that we are all made holy and united to God by his gift of *sanctifying* grace, but God also gives special, *gratuitous* graces to some people to enable them to help lead others toward union with him. Thomas builds on St. Paul's list of gratuitous graces in 1 Corinthians 12:8–10: "To one is given through the Spirit the utterance of *wisdom*, and to another the utterance of *knowledge* according to the same Spirit, to another *faith* by the same Spirit, to another gifts of *healing* by the one Spirit, to another the working of *miracles*, to another *prophecy*, to another the *ability to distinguish between spirits*, to another various kinds of *tongues*, to another the *interpretation of tongues*."[154]

---

[154] RSV; italics added for emphasis.

Thomas classes these various gifts into three categories, noting, "It must be observed that some of them pertain to knowledge, some to speech, and some to operation."[155]

Graces pertaining to knowledge all relate in some manner to *prophecy*, and prophecies may relate to matters of *faith, wisdom, discernment of spirits,* or *knowledge* (as we'll flesh out in just a minute). Graces pertaining to speech are the abilities to *speak in tongues* or to *interpret tongues.* Graces pertaining to operation are the gifts of *healing* and *miracle working.* Let's take a minute now to look at the miraculous ways in which all these graces work.

Can we foresee the future without God's gift of prophecy?

As beings with rational powers, there is a limited sense in which we can "see" the future. After all, haven't you ever told someone, "I told you so!" when he took some harmful action after you warned him what would happen? In our daily lives, we strive to understand cause-and-effect relationships in the workings of the world so we can predict, and sometimes even control, what happens in the future. Such is the business of the virtue of prudence. These too are the goals of science and technology.

Prophecy, however, is something altogether beyond these natural processes. It is a direct gift from God whereby the prophet foretells future events beyond human knowledge, and pronounces them with certainty, since what he sees comes not from the light of his natural powers of sensation and reason, but through the direct and infused light of God. Thomas cites the

[155] *ST*, II-II, Q. 171, prologue.

prophet Micah (7:8) here: *"When I sit in darkness, the Lord is my light."*[156]

Prophecy is not only about future events, but may also concern past and present events that are "remote from our knowledge."[157] Moses, the greatest human prophet, was granted prophetic knowledge by God to write about the beginning of the world. Prophecies regarding the future may be prophecies of *denunciation* whereby the prophet predicts what will happen *if* certain actions are not taken; for example, hazards that will follow if a people does not repent, and prophecies of *foreknowledge* predict things not dependent upon the actions of man's free will that are predestined by God to occur. Prophecies relating to things we all should believe pertain to matters of *faith*, those relating to higher mysteries pertain to *wisdom*, those relating to good or evil spiritual substances pertain to *discernment of spirits*, and those relating to the guidance of human actions pertain to *knowledge*.

Habes gratiam linguarum?

("Do you have the gift of tongues?") We learn in Acts 2 that on the day of Pentecost, the Holy Spirit descended upon those gathered in the Upper Room and produced tongues of fire over each of their heads, and they began to speak in languages unknown to them before. Thomas tells us this gift serves Christ's great commission, "according to Matt. 28:19, *Going . . . teach ye all nations.*"[158] God provided Christ's first disciples with this special capacity to speak in and understand the languages of a

---

[156] *ST*, II-II, Q. 171, art. 2.
[157] Ibid., art. 3.
[158] *ST*, II-II, Q. 176, art. 1.

variety of nations so they could go forth to spread the Gospel to the poor and the powerless in places where they could not find others to interpret their own language and explain their messages to those in foreign lands filled with unbelievers. In other words, God supplied them with the tools for the job that he assigned them. And to see how effectively they got that job done, we need only recall the words that St. Augustine wrote less than four centuries later: "Whereas even now the Holy Ghost is received, yet no one speaks in the tongues of all nations, because the Church herself already speaks the languages of all nations."[159]

Why does God give the grace of miracles?

Through the gratuitous grace of miracles, God uses man as his instrument to produce wondrous events beyond the powers of nature. Miracles are called signs, and their primary purpose is to confirm with certainty the knowledge brought to people's attention by other gratuitous graces like prophecy and the gift of tongues. Thomas tells us that "the common benefit of miracles" is "the bringing of men to the knowledge of God."[160]

[159] ST, II-II, Q. 176, art. 1.
[160] ST, II-II, Q. 178, art. 1.

CHAPTER NINETEEN

Are You a Thinker or a Doer?

Accordingly, since certain men are especially intent on the contemplation of truth, while others are especially intent on external actions, it follows that man's life is fittingly divided into active and contemplative.

—ST, II-II, Q. 179, art. 1

After having considered differences among people in terms of the special graces some receive, Thomas examines differences in the types of lives that Christians may be called to live. These primary callings are to the *contemplative* life, where a person focuses on the inward contemplation of truth, and the *active* life, where he focuses on external actions and affairs in the world. I think of such people as *thinkers* and *doers* (and *lovers* as well).[161]

---

[161] See also my *Three Irish Saints: A Guide to Finding Your Spiritual Style* (Charlotte, NC: TAN Books, 2012). It builds upon Thomas's analysis of the contemplative and active lives, portraying St. Kevin of Glendalough as an exemplary contemplative "thinker," St. Patrick of Ireland as a model active "doer," and St. Brigid of Kildare as an ideal active "lover" by dividing the active style of life into *doers* who act on a broad scale and *lovers* best known for their personal acts of charity. We might all ask ourselves whether we are primarily thinkers, doers, or

These categories derive from the very nature of the human intellectual soul. "The life of plants consists of nourishment and generation; the life of animals of sensation and movement; and the life of men in their understanding and acting according to reason."[162] God gave us the capacities to *know* truth and to *act* for good. We see this in the two main functions of our reasoning powers. By the workings of our *speculative* intellect, we contemplate truths and are perfected by the intellectual virtues of understanding, science, and reason. By the workings of our *practical* intellect, we get things done and are perfected by the virtues of art and prudence.

What do holy thinkers think?

Christian contemplatives are thinkers indeed, but they are far from professional academics or cool "Mr. Spock" types who analyze the world with reason alone in detachment from the truths they seek. Indeed, contemplatives seek the highest truths of God, and their wills are fired by their love for him. As Thomas notes, "There is delight in the contemplative life, not only by reason of the contemplation itself, but also by reason of the Divine love."[163] Citing St. Gregory the Great, he expands on this theme: "The contemplative life is sweetness exceedingly lovable; for it carries the soul away above itself, it opens heaven and discovers the spiritual world to the eyes of the mind."[164] Contemplation of God is a foretaste of the eternal bliss of the beatific vision of God, although in a very imperfect

---

lovers, and what we might learn from others with our own or with different "spiritual styles."

[162] *ST*, II-II, Q. 179, art. 1.
[163] *ST*, II-II, Q. 180, art. 7.
[164] *ST*, II-II, Q. 181, art. 7.

form here on earth — "for the contemplation of wayfarers is imperfect, according to 1 Cor. 13:12, *We see now through a glass in a dark manner.*"[165] It will be perfect in heaven when we see God "face to face" (1 Cor. 13:12).

Four things necessary to the contemplative life are obtained in this order: 1) *moral virtues*, which must be attained so we will not be disturbed by our passions or outward events and will be free to focus on truth; 2) *intellectual preparation* in the form of acts such as focusing our attention, studying, and reasoning, to set the stage for contemplation; 3) *contemplation of divine effects*, that is, of creatures and the workings of the world God created, which paves the way toward the final step: 4) *contemplation of the divine truth of God*, the origin and sustainer of all of creation. A contemplative soul sees the goodness and beauty of God in even the least of his creatures, and when his eye sees the creature, his mind and his heart rise to the Creator.

What do holy doers do?

God has given us the capacity not only to know the truth, but to do the good. In Aristotle's terms, he has made us not only "rational animals," but "political animals" too. We live together in communities and are called to look after each other's welfare. As Christ told us, we are to love our neighbors as ourselves, and this suggests that we take actions for our neighbors' good. This is particularly the stuff of the moral virtues.

The moral virtues are geared toward action, and as Thomas notes: "The chief of the moral virtues is justice, by which one man is directed in his relations towards another."[166] So then,

---

[165] *ST*, II-II, Q. 180, art. 7.
[166] *ST*, II-II, Q. 181, art. 1.

"when we practice the works of the moral virtues as being good in themselves, and not as dispositions to the contemplative life, the moral virtues belong to the active life."[167] Prudence, that blend of intellectual and moral virtue that gets things done, is "*right reason applied to action*"[168] and is therefore a quintessential virtue of the active life.

For a sample of the kinds of actions that those of the active life are called to do, I direct readers to St. Thomas's excellent consideration of the spiritual and corporal works of mercy in his article "Of Almsdeeds," in question 32 of the Second Part of the Second Part of the *Summa Theologica*. In this part of the *Summa*, Thomas focuses attention on one particular act of the active life that might at first glance seem contemplative; this is the act of *teaching*. The teacher must indeed contemplate truths and acquire wisdom. Indeed, a sure sign that someone possesses wisdom and knowledge is his ability to teach others. Even when he shares those fruits of his contemplation, it is the work of the active life as well.

Thinking vs. doing: which one wins?

In one sense it is a false matchup to pit the two kinds of life against each other, since, although some of us are especially disposed to one or the other, we are all called to some extent to think about God and to do good things. Thomas draws heavily on the writings of St. Gregory the Great in his comparisons of the contemplative and active lives.[169] In using an example from

---

[167] *ST*, II-II, Q. 181, art. 1.
[168] *ST*, II-II, Q. 181, art. 2; citing Aristotle's *Nichomachean Ethics*, bk. 5, chap. 2.
[169] Gregory himself was a fascinating example of a man who by inclination was a contemplative hermit and yet was called by

the Old Testament, Gregory wrote that Jacob's wife Leah, who was "blear-eyed" (Gen. 29:17) but fruitful, "signifies the active life; which being occupied with work, sees less, and yet since it urges one's neighbor both by word and example to its imitation, begets a number of offspring of good deeds."[170] Gregory adds, "*The contemplative life gives beauty to the soul*, wherefore it is signified by Rachel, of *whom* it is said (Gen. 29:17) that she was *of a beautiful countenance*."

The most famous biblical example is that of Martha, representing the active life, and her sister Mary, the contemplative. Jesus declared, "Martha, Martha, thou art careful, and art troubled about many things: But one thing is necessary. Mary hath chosen the best part, which shall not be taken away from her." (Luke 10:41–42). Here we see Christ's acknowledgment of the value of contemplation. Gregory would say: "Great are the merits of the active life, but greater still those of the contemplative."[171] Thomas would note as well that the contemplative part will not be taken away, since our eternal bliss will consist in the beatific vision of God himself.

God to the emphatically active office of the papacy. So well did he pursue that active life that he became one of a handful of popes to be called "the Great." And yet he lamented the loss of his contemplative focus on heavenly things. "But now," he wrote while pope, "by reason of my pastoral charge, my poor soul is enforced to endure the burden of secular men's business, and after so sweet a kind of rest" (Edmund G. Gardner, ed., *The Dialogues of St. Gregory the Great* [Mercantville, NJ: Evolution Press, 2010], 4).

[170] *ST*, II-II, Q. 182, art. 1; citing Gregory's *Homily on Ezekiel*.
[171] *ST*, II-II, Q. 182, art. 2.

CHAPTER TWENTY

Your Particular Gifts

> It is written in praise of the Church (Ps. 44:10) that she
> is surrounded with variety; and a gloss on these words says
> that the Queen, namely the Church, is bedecked with the
> teaching of the Apostles, the confessions of martyrs, the
> purity of virgins, the sorrowing of penitents.
>
> —ST, II-II, Q. 183, art. 2

What are the states of God's union?

When Thomas completed his study of the virtues common
to all, he began his treatises on things of God pertaining to
some people and not to others. After explaining the need to
examine the gratuitous graces and the differences between the
contemplative and active life, he noted: "A third difference
corresponds to the various duties and states of life, as expressed
in Eph. 4:11, *And He gave some apostles; and some prophets; and
other some evangelists; and other some pastors and doctors*; and
this pertains to diversity of ministries, of which it is written
(1 Cor. 12:5): *There are diversities of ministries*."[172] While the
Church is one, she is perfected in her unity by people playing
many different roles. Though God's own perfection is simple

---

[172] *ST*, II-II, Q. 171, prologue.

and uniform,[173] it exists in the universe "in a multiform and manifold manner, so too, the fullness of grace, which is centered in Christ as head, flows forth to His members in various ways, for the perfection of the Church."[174]

States of life may differ in terms of their approach to spiritual *perfection* (beginners, the proficient, and the perfect); in terms of the *actions or duties* of those in various states, such as married people, secular priests, or members of religious orders; and in terms of the *order of ecclesiastical beauty* seen in the hierarchical arrangement of the offices of the Church.

Can we attain the state of perfection?

Yes, in at least two senses. Jesus himself told us, "Be you therefore perfect, as also your heavenly father is perfect" (Matt. 5:48). We've seen that our final end of eternal happiness will consist in union with God. This, our ultimate perfection, *is a perfection built upon love*: "Now it is charity that unites us to God, Who is the last end of the human mind, since *he that abideth in charity abideth in God and God in him* (1 John 4:16)."[175] Our ultimate perfection will come only in heaven, but we can attain a degree of perfection during our life on earth, as we grow in the love of God that binds us more closely to him. Charity, Thomas tells us, increases in a way analogous to growth in human development, from the incapacities of infancy to the manifold powers of full maturity. Its growth can be seen in three stages or degrees of perfection.

[173] Stay tuned for Thomas's explanation, coming soon, in chapters 23 and 24.
[174] *ST*, II-II, Q. 183, art. 2.
[175] *ST*, II-II, Q. 184, art. 1.

Beginners are infants in the spirit, and their focus is primarily on *the avoidance of sin*, battling urges of the myriad earthly desires that remove our hearts and minds from God. *Proficients* at the second degree of development of charity are consumed in the *pursuit of virtue*: "In second place, man's chief pursuit is to aim at progress in good, and this is the pursuit of the proficient, whose chief aim is to strengthen their charity, by adding to it."[176] Although pursuing virtue is a noble and efficacious means of squelching sin, proficients must still continue to fight the good fight against their sinful natures. Thomas quite graphically compares this task to those who built the walls of Jerusalem while fighting off their enemies: "with one of his hands he did the work, and with the other he held a sword" (Neh. 4:17).

The *perfect* "aim chiefly at union with and enjoyment of God" and *"desire to be dissolved and to be with Christ."*[177]

How, then, can we grow perfect?

Jesus told us: "If you love me, keep my commandments" (John 14:15). And what are his commandments? The greatest commandments are these: "Jesus said to him: Thou shalt love the Lord thy God with thy whole heart, and with thy whole soul, and with thy whole mind. This is the greatest and the first commandment. And the second is like to this: Thou shalt love thy neighbour as thyself. On these two commandments dependeth the whole law and the prophets" (Matt. 22:37–40). St.

---

[176] *ST*, II-II, Q. 24, art. 9.

[177] Ibid. (It is reported that when Christ once appeared to St. Thomas, he told him he had written well and asked what reward he would like. The Angelic Doctor's perfect answer was "Only you, Lord.")

Thomas sums it up like this: "Primarily and essentially the perfection on the Christian life consists in charity, principally as to the love of God, secondarily as to the love of our neighbor, both of which are the matter of the Divine law . . . Consequently, it is evident that perfection consists in the observance of the commandments."[178]

We grow toward perfection when we act as God has commanded us, including following the Ten Commandments — which remove us from things that are opposed to the love of charity. Christ's great commandments are commandments of charity itself. The special *counsels* of those in religious life (*poverty, chastity, obedience* to superiors) are special aids that help remove obstacles that are not directly opposed to charity (such as marriage and business concerns), but which can hinder acts of charity by diverting attention toward worldly matters.

Thomas also writes extensively about the special state of perfection to which bishops are called and notes, "Bishops are busy about things pertaining to the love of their neighbor, arising out of the abundance of their love of God. Hence our Lord asked Peter first of all whether he loved him, and afterwards committed the care of His flock to him."[179]

[178] *ST*, II-II, Q. 184, art. 3.
[179] Ibid., art. 8.

DUMB OX BOX #6
Does science hinder or help our devotion to God?

Hear Thomas's warning: "Science and anything conducive to greatness is to man an occasion of self-confidence, so that he does not wholly surrender himself to God. The result is that such like things sometimes occasion a hindrance to devotion." And yet: "If, however, a man perfectly submits to God his science or any other perfection, by this fact his very devotion is increased" (*ST*, II-II, Q. 83, art. 3).

So, as we rightly strive to develop our God-given capacities to acquire knowledge and develop all of our powers, we should not get too big for our britches by forgetting him who gave us those powers in the first place.

Thomas talks about this in the context of devotion, which is one of the "interior acts" of the virtue of religion. Interior acts are mental, in contrast with such "exterior acts" as genuflecting, giving tithes, singing God's praises, or making vows to God or oaths in his name. Thomas notes, "Devotion is an act of will whereby a man offers himself for the service of God" (*ST*, II-II, Q. 82, art. 1). *Devout* persons devote themselves to God in such a way that all of their actions will be directed toward the will of God.

And as for science, we have seen that the word comes from "*scire*" ("to know"), and in Thomas's writings it is synonymous with *knowledge*. I used the word *science* for this question because in our day there are some rather prominent and knowledgeable scientists who illustrate both the potential pitfalls and potential advantages that human knowledge can provide.

PART II

God

---

*Moses said to God: "Lo, I shall go to the
children of Israel, and say to them: 'The God
of your fathers hath sent me to you.' If they should
say to me: 'What is his name?' what shall I say
to them?" God said to Moses: "I AM WHO AM."
He said: "Thus shalt thou say to the children
of Israel: 'HE WHO IS, hath sent me to you.'"*

—Exodus 3:13–14

CHAPTER TWENTY-ONE

How to Think about God

We shall try, by God's help, to set forth whatever is included in this Sacred Science as briefly and clearly as the matter itself may allow.

—ST, prologue

Having addressed the nature of humanity in Part I, I hope your mental muscles are thoroughly warmed up, *for now the real workout begins.* We dive next into the deepest of waters — those of the mysterious, unfathomable nature of God himself. We move now from creature to Creator; from us, who are made in the image and likeness of God, to the God whose limitless greatness we reflect in such a small and limited way. We struggle next with the sublime themes and ideas that Thomas presented "in such a way as may tend to the instruction of beginners"[180] from the very first pages of the *Summa Theologica* itself, in that book's Part I.

It is much easier to talk about mankind than about God, since we all possess some truly inside information about at least one person — namely, ourselves! We also know plenty of others through the direct evidence of our senses. Although God gave us those senses, plus all we will ever perceive through them,

[180] ST, prologue.

we can see God only "through a mirror dimly," while here on earth, but when in heaven "then face to face" (1 Cor. 13:12, RSV). While Thomas was here on earth, he polished that mirror as few have before or since. He knew so well the wise words that "for by the greatness of the beauty, and of the creature, the creator of them may be seen, so as to be known thereby" (Wisd. 13:5). So, let's set our powers of attention and intellect on high as we seek to absorb some small sense of the greatness and beauty of the Creator that Thomas saw reflected all around him, in all that He created—through the "sacred science" of God, which is theology.

What ten things should we know about theology, the sacred science of God?

1. Theology *is necessary*, in addition to philosophy. Theology is based upon the revealed teachings of God. Although philosophy can discover some truths about God, it does so in a gradual and limited way. God's revelation teaches us truths that exceed human reason and help guide us toward salvation.

2. Theology *is a kind of science*. Although the articles of faith are not self-evident and some people deny them, some sciences depend on principles known by a higher science. As musicians accept principles taught by mathematicians, so theology is established upon principles revealed directly by God.

3. Theology *is one, unified science* or body of knowledge. Although it studies creatures and the Creator, angels, corporeal beings, and human morality, it studies God

primarily and created beings only insofar as they relate to God as their beginning or end, their source or their goal.

4. Theology *is primarily a speculative, rather than a practical science*, because its primary aim is *knowledge* about God, rather than human *acts*. Still, it is both speculative and practical, in helping man toward his salvation, in which he will attain the perfect knowledge of God (the beatific vision), which will provide eternal bliss.

5. Theology *is the highest and noblest of sciences.* "Wisdom sent her maids to invite to the tower" (Prov. 9:3). Other sciences are the handmaids of theology. Theology is higher and nobler than other sciences because its truths are more certain, being based upon God's revelation, and because its subject matter is of the highest worth, its subject being God.

6. Theology *is wisdom above all human wisdom.* Wisdom orders and judges things according to higher principles, as the architect who plans a house is wiser than the laborers who assemble the wood or the stones. God is the architect and highest cause of the whole universe, so the study of God is the highest of wisdom.

7. Theology's *object is God.* As noted in point 3, in the sacred science of theology, all things in the universe are studied as they relate to God as their origin and their end.

8. Theology *rightly uses arguments.* It does not argue to prove articles held by faith, but it does use these articles to prove other things, as St. Paul argues from the resurrection of Christ to demonstrate the truth of the

general resurrection (1 Cor. 15). Arguments from human authority are the weakest; arguments from divine revelation are the strongest.

9. *Holy Scripture rightly uses metaphors* because comparisons with material things help us to comprehend spiritual truths. Further, some things taught metaphorically in some parts of scripture are taught more directly in other parts.

10. *Holy Scripture has multiple levels of meaning.* Within the same sentence, it can describe a fact and reveal a mystery. God can signify things not only in words, as men do, but also by things and events themselves. Interpretations should start at the *historical* or *literal* sense. Based upon the literal level is the *spiritual sense*, whereby things signified by words signify other things still. Within the spiritual sense, things of the Old Law that signify or point to things of the New Law constitute the *allegorical sense*. Things that signify what we ought to do and how we are to live constitute the *moral sense*. Things that relate to or point to eternal glory constitute the *analogical sense*.

Is God's existence self-evident to us?

Some people argue that the existence of God is self-evident and undeniable because of one or more of the following: 1) knowledge of God is implanted in us by nature;[181] 2) as soon as the statement "God exists" is understood, his existence cannot

[181] Here Thomas cites St. John Damascene's *On the Exposition of the Orthodox Faith*, I, 2, 3.

be denied, because the word *God* means that thing than which nothing greater can be thought, but what exists in reality is greater than that which exists only mentally;[182] or 3) the existence of truth is self-evident and cannot be denied. If truth does not exist, then the statement "Truth does not exist" is *true*. But God *is* the truth (and the way and the life), per John 14:6.

And yet the Philosopher (Aristotle) notes that we cannot mentally admit the opposite of what is self-evident,[183] but people do deny that God exists, and as Scripture tells us, "The fool said in his heart: There is no God" (Ps. 52:1). God's existence *would be* self-evident to us *if* God's essence were understood (since, as we will see in a few pages, his existence and essence are one), but God's essence is imperfectly known to man, and our imperfect knowledge is achieved through reasoned argument or through revelation.

An awareness of God is implanted in our natures, but in a very confused way. It is one thing to know that *someone* approaches and another thing to know that it is (for example) Peter. All men seek happiness, but not all realize that our complete happiness (beatitude) lies only in God. Further, to *mentally grasp the idea* of a being than whom nothing greater can be imagined does not prove that such a being *actually exists*. In fact, we know there are people who will not admit that God exists.

Finally, that truth in general exists is self-evident; this cannot be rationally denied. Yet the existence of one Primal Truth who is God is *not* self-evident to us.

---

[182] Most notably proposed by St. Anselm of Canterbury, although St. Thomas does not name him.

[183] For example, that a part is greater than the whole, or that 1 + 1 does not make 2.

Can God's existence be proven?[184]

Some people argue that the existence of God cannot be proven through reason because of one of more of the following: 1) God's existence is an article of faith, and "faith is of the unseen" (Heb. 11:1) and not amenable to scientific demonstration. 2) To argue that God exists, we must understand his essence, what he really *is*, but we are capable of only understanding what God is *not*,[185] or 3) God's existence can only be inferred from his effects—but his effects, which are finite, are not like him, who is infinite.

And yet, as St. Paul wrote, "For the invisible things of him, from the creation of the world, are clearly seen, being understood by the things that are made" (Rom. 1:20). It is valid to reason *a posteriori*—that is, from things already known to us—to things not yet known. We can see and know the effects of God and then reason from them to demonstrate his existence as their cause—because if an effect exists, we know that its cause must have preceded it. Things about God that we can derive from reason, such as his existence, are not themselves articles of faith, but are *preambles* or starting points to the faith. Faith presupposes natural knowledge, grace presupposes nature, and perfection presupposes something to be perfected.[186] We also need not comprehend the essence of *what God is*, to demonstrate *that*

---

[184] In 1870, the First Vatican Council would declare as dogma that certain knowledge of God can be attained through "the light of reason."

[185] Citing St. John Damascene's *On the Exposition of the Orthodox Faith*, I, 4 (and denoting the "negative theology" we'll examine a little later).

[186] Although indeed, those who cannot mentally grasp a proof may rightly accept on faith things that can be proven.

God exists, because the question of what something is comes after the question of its existence. We need only know things about God's effects in order to demonstrate his existence. Finally, although God immeasurably exceeds his effects, and in no way can we come to know God perfectly through the study of his effects, those effects do demonstrate that he exists as their ultimate cause.

CHAPTER TWENTY-TWO

God Exists

The existence of God can be proved in five ways.

—*ST*, I, Q. 2, art. 3

What are five ways to prove the existence of God?[187]

The argument from motion: Our senses tell us with certainty that some things are in motion. They change in various ways, such as in their location or in a quality such as temperature. They move from some kind of state of *potentiality* to an *actuality*. Anything that moves from a potentiality to an actuality must be made actual by something outside of itself. A thing cannot *give* what it does not already *have*. These outside sources of change cannot go on indefinitely, though, so there must be a first agent of change, a First Mover to put the series of

---

[187] Countless authors have spent countless minutes examining the few paragraphs in the *Summa Theologica* in which St. Thomas lays out his five logical demonstrations that lead us to God's existence. St. Thomas provides merely summaries in the *Summa Theologica*, but has laid out arguments for God in much greater detail in the first part of his *Summa Contra Gentiles*.

changes in motion, as a stick moves something else only because it is put in motion by a hand. There must be a first, unmoved mover, already completely actualized and put in motion by no other. This mover we call God.

The argument from efficient cause: Our senses reveal an order of efficient causes by examining which effects are produced. A thing cannot cause itself, because then it would exist prior to itself, which is impossible. The chain of causation cannot go into infinity because without a first cause, no intermediate causes would exist, and to take away the cause is to take away the effect. But there are effects. Therefore, there must be a first efficient cause, and this we call God.

The argument from necessary being: We find in nature things that are possible to be or not to be, things that come to be, but pass away. If everything is possible not to be, at one time there could have been no existing thing. If that were true, there would be nothing now, because something that does not exist cannot give itself its own existence. There must therefore be some being that not merely *possibly*, but *necessarily* exists, having received its existence not from another thing, but which causes other things to exist. We call this necessary being God.

The argument from degrees of being: Everything that exists has some measure of goodness by the fact that it exists. Still, we clearly see that some things in the world are better than others. They are more good, noble, true, or complete. But there is no standard to appreciate degrees of perfection unless there is an unchanging maxi-mum. There must be some utmost being that causes the goodness and various perfections in every other being. This ultimate being and source of all perfections we call God.

The argument from the governance of the world:[188] There is order and seemingly purposeful behavior even in inanimate natural bodies that follow the regular laws of nature. Although they lack awareness, they act in the same way, over and over again, in ways that achieve ef-fective ends or goals. Unintelligent beings cannot reach specific goals unless directed by a being with intelli-gence, "as the arrow is shot to its mark by the archer. Therefore, some intelligent being exists by whom all natural things are directed to their end; and this being we call God."[189]

Why do some modern scientists have problems with the five ways?

St. Thomas prefaces his brief summary of the five ways to demonstrate God's existence by noting two objections. The first is an argument attempting to disprove God's existence by evidence of the existence of evil. To put it in brief: since God is infinite goodness, if he exists, there would be no evil in the

---

[188] St. Thomas refers to this as the "argument from the gover-nance of the world." Many today call this argument based on purposeful behavior the "argument from design," and as we will see in a few pages, it is also known as the "argument from final cause."

[189] ST, I, Q. 2, art. 3.

Ways to God Arguments from:	Aspects of God	The Five Starting Points in the World of the Senses
Motion	Prime Mover or Unmoved Mover	Movement or change
Effects	Efficient Cause	Effects
Necesary being	Necessary Being	Contingent beings or possible things
Degrees of being	Perfection of Being	Varying degrees of goodness
Governance of the world	Final Cause	Ordered and purposeful behavior

world, but there is evil in the world, so God does not exist. St. Thomas responds, citing St. Augustine, that God allows evils to exist, since in his omnipotence, he can produce goodness even out of evil.[190]

A second objection holds that "it is superfluous to suppose that what can be accounted for by a few principles has been

---

[190] What greater example than Christ's crucifixion?

Ways to God

Key Statements

What moves is moved by something else. Motion is reduction of something from *potentiality* to *actuality*. This reduction can occur only by something in the state of *actuality*.

No effect is the cause of itself, for to be so it would be prior to it-self. There can be no effects at all without a *first efficient cause*.

Things in nature can exist or not. They cannot exist always. If they can be nonexistent, at one time there could be nothing, and also nothing now. *That which does not exist only begins to exist by something already extant.*

Among beings there are some more and some less *good*, true, noble and the like. But more and less are judged of different things, according as they *resemble* in their different ways, something which is the maximum.

Things that lack intelligence *act for an end*. Whatever lacks intelligence cannot move toward an end, unless it is *directed by some being endowed with knowledge and intelligence.*

produced by many."[191] The idea of God is unneeded because natural things can be explained by the one principle of nature and voluntary things by the principle of human reason or will.

[191] Although well-known to St. Thomas, and indeed to think-ers millennia before him, such as Aristotle and Ptolemy, this principle for preferring the simplest theories with the fewest assumptions is popularly called "Ockham's razor," after Cath-olic philosopher William of Ockham (c. 1285–1349).

Thomas replies that, as was shown in the body of the article on the fifth way, nature acts for ends under the direction of that *final end* which is God. And as for human reason and will, these too are imperfect and changeable and "must be traced back to an immovable and self-necessary first principle."[192]

Readers should also take note that some modern critics of the five ways suppose they are based on a primitive, prescientific, Aristotelian, "teleological" or goal-directed view of nature that has been supplanted by modern science with its mechanistic, deterministic understanding of the mindless workings of nature. Ironically, Aristotle and Aquinas saw their teleological understanding as an advance upon mechanist, deterministic world-views of the very ancient pre-Socratic philosophers, who wrote before the development of a mature metaphysics or philosophy of the nature of being. The pre-Socratics, like modern adherents of scientism, consider merely *efficient* causation (that *by which* things come about), ignoring or dismissing the implications of *material* causation (that *out of which* things derive), formal causation (that *into which* things become), and final causation (that *for the sake of which* things happen). And even in their consideration of efficient causes, they do not see that reason demands a *first* efficient cause.[193]

Please know too that most pagan Greek philosophers, including Aristotle, believed the universe itself was not created,

---

[192] *ST*, I, Q. 2, art. 3.

[193] For an intriguing analysis of this irony, see Timothy McDermott's *Summa Theologiae: A Concise Translation* (Notre Dame, IN: Christian Classics from Ave Maria Press, 1991), xxiii–xxv. For a masterful exposition of teleology, including the analysis of "form and matter" and of the five ways, see Edward Fesser's *Aquinas: A Beginner's Guide* (Oxford: Oneworld, 2009).

but existed always. St. Thomas believed that *reason alone* could *not* decide the issue either way. We know, as an article of faith, that the universe was created because God himself has revealed it to us in Scripture.[194] Therefore, Thomas crafted the five ways to demonstrate that God must exist, *even if the universe always existed with him*. (Can you wrap your mind around that one?!) Even if the universe was not *created* in time, the universe could not be *sustained* in existence without the causal power of God! The five ways are not dependent merely upon time. The great chains of causation are *not* based on the impossibility of a chronological regress. All movement or change, causation, perfection, order, and purpose, require a prime mover, first efficient cause, necessary being, ultimate formal cause, and final cause for their existence, not merely sometime in the past, but *at this very moment*.

"We live, and move, and are"[195] *right now* through the grace, love, and power of an eternal God.

---

[194] How wondrous that modern science unknown to Aquinas also lends support for creation in the "big bang" theory.

[195] Acts 17:28. St. Paul cites this line from the ancient Cretan philosopher/poet Epimenides.

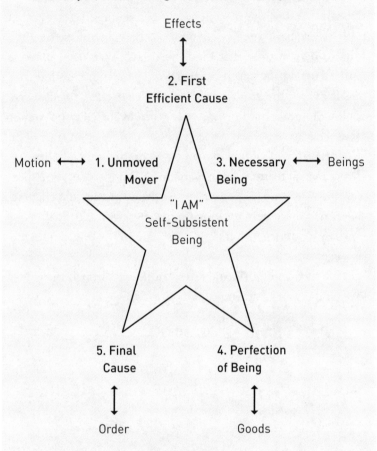

A Simple, Stellar Diagram of the Five Ways to God

Effects

2. First
Efficient Cause

Motion ←→ 1. Unmoved   3. Necessary ←→ Beings
Mover   Being

"I AM"
Self-Subsistent
Being

5. Final   4. Perfection
Cause   of Being

Order   Goods

They are *five* related paths to the *one* and only God. Everything
that emanates from God points back to His existence.
It must be said that every being in any way existing is from God.
— *ST*, I, Q. 44, art.1
He made the stars also.
—Genesis 1:16

CHAPTER TWENTY-THREE

What Is God *Not*?

Because we cannot know what God is, but rather
what he is not, we have no means for considering
how God is, but rather how He is not.

—*ST*, I, Q. 3, prologue

Now we consider the difference between knowing *that* God is
and knowing *what* God is or is not—and what a difference that
makes! Having established through the five ways, based on the
evidence of effects in the world that a being we call God *must
exist*, we are still faced with that all-important question Thomas
so famously posed as a child: *What is God?* How startling it is,
as we saw above, that a mature Thomas would write, "Because
we cannot know what God is, but rather what He is not, we
have no means for considering how God is, but rather how He
is not." This method for thinking about God is called the *via
negativa* ("negative way") of theology.

Thomas starts his examination of God with this way of ne-
gation to help us know some very important things about *what
God is not* by considering some attributes that could not possibly describe a Prime Mover, a Necessary Being who is pure
act. In proving, for example, that God is in no way complex
or composed of any kind of parts, we achieve some sense of

his utter *simplicity*. In proving that he cannot change, we see that his must be *immutable*. The insights we attain are never complete, though, not here on earth, and not even in heaven, when we shall see God face-to-face in the beatific vision. Even then, God's utter vastness exceeds beyond measure the comprehension of even the glorified human intellect. Let's see what light Thomas's glorious intellect can shine for us on the divine attributes of God.

What can reason tell us about five fundamental attributes of God?

Simplicity: How intriguing that while some modern atheists attack the idea of God because he would have to be so unimaginably *complex*,[196] Thomas, using the negative way, concludes that God's first fundamental attribute is his utter *simplicity*. This simplicity can be seen in many ways (that are not so simple to explain in brief).

God is not composed of body and spirit. He has no body. Scripture tells us "God is a spirit" (John 4:24) and reason tells us, "No body is in motion unless it be put in motion."[197] God is the First and Unmoved Mover. Scriptural references to God's size or to body parts like his arm or hand are metaphorical references to his vastness, power, et cetera.

God is not a composite of matter and form, because matter is a potential that is made actual by form, and God has no potential, being pure act: "Whatever is primarily and essentially an agent must be primarily and essentially form. Now God is the

---

[196] Dawkins, *The God Delusion*, 176–180.
[197] *ST*, I, Q. 3, art. 1.

first agent, since He is the first efficient cause. He is therefore of His essence a form; and not composed of matter and form."[198]

God is not separate from his nature or essence. You, reader, are a man or a woman, but not *humanity* itself, because you have your own particular matter that is your body, and God, as we saw, has no body. God is identical to his nature or essence in a way that no creature can be. "God is his very Godhead."[199]

God does not have a separate essence and existence, although it is one thing for us to know *that* God exists and quite another to know *what* he is (his *essence*). The two are the same in him. Existence is what makes potential things actual or real. Essences like humanity are called actual because they exist. Existence is to essence as actuality is to potentiality. "Therefore, since in God there is no potentiality . . . it follows that his essence does not differ from existence. Therefore, his essence is his existence."[200]

God is not contained in a genus. God cannot be classed as a particular kind of any group or category. Members of a class share the same essence, but differ in some manner of their existence, but God's essence and existence are one.

There are no accidents in God. Accidents refer to particular characteristics that can exist only in other things, such as the lush body and vibrant color of your hair. In a sense, accidental characteristics make actual or real the potential that is your hair. God forbid, such delightful attributes could change over time, and your hair would be different, but your hair would still be your hair (until the day it might give way to but a shiny

[198] Ibid., art. 2.
[199] Ibid., art. 3.
[200] *ST,* I, Q. 3, art. 4.

dome). Well, God has no accidental qualities at all, because, as we've seen so many times before, there is no potential in God, there is nothing lacking in him, nothing that could be added to actualize him, because he is already pure act. Even all these attributes are not accidents that God *has*, but descriptions of what God *is*.[201]

God is not complex in any way. He is absolutely simple. We have listed above many ways already in which God is simple, lacking bodily parts, lacking separation from his essence, lacking differentiation in his essence and existence, et cetera. "Therefore," Thomas notes, "it is clear that God is nowise composite, but is altogether simple."[202] He then provides four more arguments, from which we'll quote only the next (since we only have a minute). He states further, "Secondly . . . every composite is posterior to its component parts, and is dependent upon them, but God is the first being, as shown above [Q. 2, art. 3]." Even though, in created things, composite things are greater than their parts, this is their nature because the essence of every created thing is to be some kind of composite, at least in that its *existence* (*the fact* that it is) differs from its *essence* (*what* it is). We have seen, though, that for God, his essence and existence are one.

God does not enter into the composition of other things. Not only does God have no parts, he is certainly not a part of anything else. Some have said, in the time of Augustine, as Thomas cites, and even now, according to New Age disciples, that God is the

---

[201] As Peter Kreeft deftly explains, "Creatures have attributes (Peter is alive), but God is His Attributes (God is life)" (*Summa of the Summa* [San Francisco: Ignatius Press, 1990], 83).

[202] *ST*, I, Q. 3, art. 7.

"world-soul" or the "soul of the highest heaven." But God does not exist *in* or *as* the universe, but is its Creator and Sustainer. Interestingly, this subject seems to have raised the ire of the normally placid Angelic Doctor himself. Here St. Thomas lists one David of Dinant by name, as one "who mostly absurdly taught that God was primary matter."[203] His pantheistic doctrine taught that matter, intellect, and God were all actually one and the same. Thomas says he could not have been more wrong: "For matter is merely potential and potentiality is absolutely posterior to actuality."[204] God, though, is pure actuality. (God only knows what was the matter with David of Dinant's intellect!)

Perfection: *God lacks any kind of imperfection.* We must recognize that "a thing is perfect in proportion to its state of actuality, because we call that perfect which lacks nothing of the mode of its perfection"[205] and God is pure act. There is no unfilled potential in God. As the Creator of all good things, there is also no perfection in any creature that God does not exceed. Because "God is the first effective cause of things, the perfections of all things must pre-exist in God in a more eminent way."[206]

Infinity: *God lacks any limitation.* Nothing is received by him. Rather, as subsistent, self-sufficient being, nothing comes before him and nothing can be added to him. God alone is without beginning, end, or boundary of any kind.

[203] Ibid., art. 8.
[204] Ibid. Something actual comes first. Only something actual can cause the fulfillment of a potential.
[205] *ST*, I, Q. 4, art. 1.
[206] Ibid., art. 2.

Causes, Ways,

Aristotle's Four Causes	St. Thomas's Five Ways
Material Cause: That *out of which* something is made.	1. Argument From **Motion (Change)**: A being that is pure act, already completely actualized, not coming out of something else, and with no potential for change, must be the starting point *out of which* everything else arises.
Efficient Cause: That *by which* something is made.	2. Argument from **Effects:** God is the first causal agent, *by which* all other secondary causes in the universe produce their effects.
	3. Argument from **Being***: God is the only *necessary and uncaused being*, the ground and sustainer of all that exist.
Formal Cause: That *into which* something is made.	4. Argument from **Perfection:** All beings with limited perfection in varying degrees reflect the total perfection (completeness) of God.
Final Cause: That *for the sake of which* something is made.	5. Argument from **Purpose:** All beings strive, whether consciously or not, *for the sake of* attaining ordered ends ordained by the Final Cause, namely, God.

*This argument appeals to the deepest foundation of being itself, from which all four causes flow. (See Aidan Nichols's *Discovering Aquinas* [Grand Rapids, MI: Eerdman's Publishing Co., 2002], 46–47.)

and Attributes

Five Primal Entitative Attributes of God

Simplicity: There is nothing partial *out of which* God is composed or could be divided. He has no potential, but is completely whole and actual, and therefore simple, not complex.

Perfection: An efficient cause is that *by which* something is perfected (made complete). God is uncaused and totally actualized or complete.

Infinity: As the *self-subsistent ground of all being*, God is unlimited, sustaining all being.

Immutability: There is nothing *into which* God can change, being perfect. He acts all together in the eternal now.

Unity: All the diverse things in the universe are ordered, *for the sake of* the one supreme Intelligence that produces their interrelations.

Immutability: *God does not change.* Scripture says so plainly. "For I am the Lord, and I change not" (Mal. 3:6). Reason shows the same. Anything that changes has a passive potential to become something different, but we have seen from many angles that God is pure act and perfectly complete.

Unity: God lacks any kind of multiplication or division. There cannot be more than one infinite being because each would lack something found in the other, and therefore, would not be infinite. We also see evidence of God's supreme oneness in the unity of the world. "For all things that exist are seen to be ordered to each other since some serve others. But things that are diverse do not harmonize in the same order, unless they are reduced thereto by one."[207] God is the One.

What other divine attributes flow forth from these five?

The seventeenth-century Spanish theologian John of St. Thomas calls the five attributes that we've addressed "primordial entitative attributes of God." They are "radical attributes pertaining to the very existence of God" that "remove from the notion of pure act."[208] He notes as well that Thomas described three "secondary entitative attributes" that follow logically from them.

Goodness: God's supreme goodness follows from his *perfection.* Goods are things that we desire, and God is the ultimate cause and fulfillment of our desires. All goodness in created

[207] *ST*, I, Q. 11, art. 3.
[208] John of St. Thomas, *Introduction to the Summa Theologiae of Thomas Aquinas*, trans. Ralph McInerny (South Bend, IN: St. Augustine's Press, 2004), 27.

What Is God *Not?*

things comes from God. While created things *possess* goodness, God *is* goodness itself.

Immensity: God's immensity follows on his *infinity* and refers to his omnipresence—the fact that he is everywhere. Scripture tells us so: "It is written, *I fill heaven and earth*" (Jer. 23:24).[209] Reason tells us that God is in everything in three ways: a) through his *essence* because he causes and sustains all things, b) through his *presence* because he sees and knows all things, and c) through his *power* because all things are subject to his rule.

Eternity: God's eternity follows from his *immutability*. Since God is unchangeable, he is not limited by time and can have no beginning or end, but partakes of eternity: "the simultaneously whole and perfect possession of interminable life."[210]

---

[209] *ST*, I, Q. 8, art. 2.
[210] *ST*, I, Q. 10, art. 1; citing Boethius, *De Consol. V—On the Consolation of Philosophy*, bk. 5.

CHAPTER TWENTY-FOUR

Who *Is* He?

I answer that, *True affirmative
propositions can be formed about God.*

—*ST*, I, Q. 13, art. 12

What's God's name? That's easy, because He Who Is told us so: "It is written that when Moses asked, *If they should say to me, What is His Name? what shall I say to them? the Lord answered him, Thus shalt thou say to them, HE WHO IS hath sent me to you* (Exod. 3:13, 14)."[211]

Thomas wrote page after page expounding with logic and metaphysics on the unfathomable, yet inescapable fact that in God alone, existence (that he is) and essence (what he is) are one. Every created being participates in the existence of God, while God alone, self-subsisting, is the source and sustainer of all that exists. Note the astounding profundity, then, of these Old Testament verses that sum it all up in one sentence — from the very mouth of the Lord! God tells Moses to call him "qui est" ("who is") in St. Thomas's Latin — "I AM WHO AM" in the Revised Standard Version of the Bible. Indeed, God tells Moses, "Say this to the people of Israel, I AM has sent me to you." God also told him, "Say to the people of Israel, 'The Lord,

---

[211] *ST*, I, Q. 13, art. 11.

the God of your fathers, the God of Abraham, the God of Isaac, and the God of Jacob, has sent me to you': this is my name for ever, and thus I am to be remembered throughout all generations" (Exod. 3:15, RSV). The "God of the Philosophers," attained through pure reason, and the "God of Abraham, Isaac, and Jacob," revealed in Holy Scripture are one. His simplicity of existence, and his eternity too, are signified in those two simple words: "I AM"—not "I was" or "I will be."

Is there anything God does not know?

Nope. Some have argued that God does not know created things as individuals, because he knows them in a general sense "according as they are in Himself . . . as in their common and universal cause . . . But this cannot be. For to know a thing in general and not in particular is to have an imperfect knowledge of it."[212]

God's knowledge, of course, is perfect and complete, so complete in fact, that he discerns "the thoughts and intentions of the heart. Neither is there any creature invisible in his sight" (Heb. 4:13, 14). Further, God not only knows us inside and out as we are today, but he knows everything that exists now, has existed in the past, will exist in the future, or could possibly exist. "Whatever therefore can be made or thought, or said by the creature, as also whatever He Himself can do, all are known to God, although they are not actual."[213] Indeed, "the present glance of God extends over all time, and to all things which exist in any time, as to objects present to Him."[214] Because God

[212] *ST*, I, 14, art. 6.
[213] Ibid., art. 9.
[214] Ibid.

is completely actual and exists in eternity, he knows things instantly and requires no steps in a cognitive process as we do in order to know things. He can see even contingent or possible future events, because his understanding is in eternity, unbounded by time. "Just as he who goes along the road, does not see those who come after him; whereas he who sees the whole road from a height, sees at once all travelling by the way,"[215] God sees all of creation from the height of eternity.

An old commercial for margarine used to warn: "It's not nice to fool Mother Nature!" (That particular margarine brand got her to think it was butter!) But it is truly God who cannot be fooled. As he told his prophet, "Before I formed thee in the bowels of thy mother, I knew thee" (Jer. 1:5).

Can God can make the past not to have been?

This is an ancient trick question, and I have used the wording (in translation) of a question asked by Thomas himself.[216] It is much akin to the modern stumper asking if God could make a boulder so heavy that even he could not lift it. We have seen that God is omniscient and truly *knows all*. But is he omnipotent? Is he truly *all-powerful*? The answer to that question is yes, although the answer to Thomas's question is no. Thomas notes, "There does not fall under the scope of God's omnipotence anything that implies a contradiction. Now, that the past should not have been implies a contradiction."[217] God is able to do all things that are noncontradictory, that is, things that

---

[215] Ibid., art. 13.
[216] *ST*, I, Q. 25, art. 4. "Videtur quod Deus possit facere quod praeterita non fuerint."
[217] Ibid.

could *possibly* be done. God is truth and cannot make an event that truly happened not happen. (The boulder question also reveals a self-contradictory view of omnipotence.) Regarding *all things possible*, there are *no limits* to God's power. He can raise the dead and create the entire glorious universe *ex nihilo* ("out of nothing").

Is God truth itself?

Yes. "Our Lord says, *I am the Way, the Truth, and the Life* (John 14:6)."[218] Truth from the human perspective is the correspondence between reality and our understanding of it, conformity between thing and thought. Not only do created things conform or correspond to God's thought, but "His act of understanding is the measure and cause of every other being and intellect." Truth does not merely exist *in* God as it can in us, but "He is truth itself, and the sovereign and first truth."[219] For us, thinking does not make it so. For God, it does!

Does the self-subsistent being really love you and me?

God's nature is so awesome and unfathomable that we can never fully comprehend him. Is it possible, then, that being itself, He Who Is, could possibly love and care for simple, fallible human beings like you and me? Well, we've seen that the Unmoved Mover, the First Cause, all-knowing and all-powerful, this "god of the philosophers," is also the God of the Scriptures, the "God of Abraham, Isaac, and Jacob" (Exod. 3:15), and as Thomas makes clear from the start in his discussion of God's

---

[218] *ST*, I, 16, art. 5.
[219] Ibid.

love: "It is written: *God is love* (John 4:16)."[220] Love is a function of the will, and God's will causes the very existence of all things, including you and me. Thomas notes as well: "It is said (Wisd. 11:15), *Thou lovest all things that are, and hatest none of the things which Thou hast made.*"[221] God displays his love to us in sustaining our very being, and in his acts of perfect justice and mercy. So, yes, God clearly loves even you and me and would have us share in eternal happiness with him.

Is God happy?

Since beatitude (happiness) is found when an intellectual nature is aware that it possesses good and controls its own actions, and God is entirely good and all-powerful, "beatitude belongs to God in the highest degree."[222] God enjoys an unfathomable bliss that encompasses, embraces, and exceeds all other beatitudes: "Whatever is desirable in whatsoever beatitude, whether true or false, pre-exists wholly in a more eminent degree in the divine beatitude."[223] How happy we will be when we share in his beatitude in heaven!

---

[220] *ST*, I, Q. 20, art. 1.
[221] Ibid., art. 2.
[222] *ST*, I, Q. 26, art. 1.
[223] Ibid., art. 4.

Was it "fitting" that Eve was made from Adam's rib?

St. Thomas poses this in the *Summa Theologica*, "The Production of the Woman." Someone had objected that a man's rib is much smaller than a woman's body—and therefore in Genesis 2:22, "the woman should have been described as made out of that which was added, rather than out of the rib itself" (*ST*, I, Q. 92, art. 3).

But Thomas recognizes the importance of the symbolic meaning of the passage. He notes that woman was not described as being made from man's head, because she was not to rule over him. She was not made from his feet, because neither was she to be held in contempt as his slave. She was made from his rib to signify their *social union*. "Secondly, for the sacramental signification; for from the side of Christ sleeping on the Cross, the sacraments flowed—namely, blood and water—on which the Church was established" (*ST*, I, Q. 92, art. 3).

As the Church, Christ's Bride, flowed from his side, so did God ordain that man's bride would come from his side, to journey with him side by side.

CHAPTER TWENTY-FIVE

The Trinity: Three Persons, One Perfection

Having considered what belongs to the unity of the divine essence, it remains to treat of what belongs to the Trinity of the persons in God.

—ST, I, Q. 27, prologue

In the first twenty-six questions of the *Summa Theologica*, Thomas explored "what belongs to the unity of the essence"[224] of God by using natural reasoning to determine what creation can tell us about its Creator. Reason tells us there is only *one* God, who is being itself, simple, perfect, unchangeable, all-powerful, and all, but this God himself, through his revelation, has told us that in a very marvelous way he is also three. Thomas believed that the reality of the God's triune nature in the Trinity *cannot be proved by reason alone.* Indeed, "whoever, then, tries to prove the trinity of the persons by natural reason, derogates from faith in two ways."[225] First off, to attempt to prove the Trinity by reason alone slights the dignity of faith, because faith pertains to "things that appear not" (Heb. 11:1), that is, to invisible,

---

[224] *ST*, I, Q. 32, art. 1.
[225] Ibid.

spiritual things that surpass the powers of our reason. Secondly, such arguments are not useful in drawing nonbelievers to the faith, since they are not conclusive in themselves and can lead nonbelievers to ridicule us if they come to think that we believe in the Trinity *because of* such arguments.

Our reasoning about the Trinity, then, is not to provide sufficient proof of the Trinity, but only to show that our belief in the triune God is not self-contradictory, is not impossible, and is reasonable—although never completely understandable. Our knowledge of the Trinity also moves us from the realm of *what* God is into the fascinating realm of *who* he is.

Who proceeds from the Father?

Although the word *trinity* does not appear in the Scriptures, multiple passages make crystal clear that God is triune, and that from the Father proceed the Son and the Holy Spirit. As for the Son, "Our Lord says, *From God I proceeded* (John 8:42)."[226] In treating of what of the Trinity of the persons in God can be grasped by our reason, building upon the revelation of Scripture, Thomas indicates we must consider three fundamental issues: first, the origin or *procession* of the persons; secondly, their *relations*; and thirdly, the *persons* themselves.

The Son and the Holy Spirit do not proceed from the Father by means of an external, outward act like that of creation. The Son and Holy Spirit are not creatures, but are God himself, and their procession is an *inward act* within God. For example, when we understand a thing in our intellects, a concept comes forth from our intellectual power and proceeds from our knowledge of that object. The concept can be signified by a

[226] *ST,* I, Q. 27, art. 1.

spoken word, becoming a "word of the voice," but it also exists unspoken within us as "the word of the heart." Procession in God is not like procession in bodies, where whatever proceeds outside is distinct from the source from which it proceeds. It is like procession in the intellect. A speaker can say a word and yet still retain its meaning within him. When we know things imperfectly, we can generate words about them. God's divine intelligence is so perfect that "the divine Word is of necessity perfectly one with the source whence he proceeds."[227]

After all, as we read in John 1:1: "In the beginning was the Word, and the Word was with God, and the Word was God." This proceeding of the Word or Son of God from the Father, akin to our acts of knowing, is the procession called "generation."

Who proceeds from the Father and the Son?

We saw that procession exists in God not in terms of an external action, like the procession of physical bodies, but in terms of an internal action, like the processes of thought that remain within the mind. The Word proceeds from God's perfect and total knowing, somewhat like the way that our concepts and words proceed from our imperfect, partial manner of knowing. But recall that our *intellects* are but one way we were formed in the image and likeness of God. The other way lies in our possession of *will*.

"The operation of the will within ourselves involves also another procession, that of love, whereby the object loved is in the lover; as, by the conception of the word, the object spoken of or understood is in the intelligent agent. Hence, besides the

---

[227] *ST*, I, Q. 27, art. 2.

procession of the Word in God, there exists in Him another procession called the procession of love."[228]

The procession of love flows from the procession of the Word, since nothing can be loved unless it is known by the intellect. We call this procession of love the Holy Spirit, and every time we recite the Nicene Creed at Mass, we declare that we believe in the Holy Spirit, "who proceeds from the Father and the Son." We saw that the Son proceeds from the Father by way of generation. A son bears a likeness to his Father. Objects that are understood reside in the intellect because our concepts bear their *likeness*, recalling that truth is conformity between things and thoughts. In a similar way, the Son bears the likeness of the Father, so the Word is described as *generated* by or *begotten* of God, although of the same substance.[229] The will does not operate based on its similarity to things willed, but according to its inclination toward them. This dynamic movement of the Father's and Son's love proceeds as spirit and is called *spiration*.

Who are God's relations?

Relationships exist when two or more distinct things can be referred to or contrasted in some way with each other. The first two of four divine relations of the Holy Spirit are the *paternity* of the Father in regard to the Son and the *filiation* (or sonship) on the part of the Son toward the Father. Some have argued that these relations don't really exist, but are only a manner of speaking, and this is the gist of the Sabellian heresy. Thomas

---

[228] *ST*, I, Q. 27, art. 3.
[229] "Begotten, not made, consubstantial with the Father" in the words of the Nicene Creed.

answers that "relations exist in God really."[230] In fact, "it is clear that in God, relation and essence do not differ from each other, but are one and the same."[231] In other words, the essence, the *quiddity* or "whatness" of God *is* the relation between the persons of the Trinity. *Being itself is relational* and there are real distinctions between the persons of God.

Paternity and *filiation* derive from the action of the intellect in the procession of the Word. The Father generates the Son, and this relation is called *paternity*. The Son is begotten by the Father, and this relation is called *filiation*. Two opposite divine relations also follow from the action of the will in which the Holy Spirit proceeds from the love of the Father and the Son. The relation of the principle of the procession of love is called *spiration*, which derives from our words for "breathing" and for "spirit." The Father and the Son *spirate* the Holy Spirit. The opposite relation, that of the spirated Holy Spirit to the Father and the Son, is called *procession*. These, then, are the four sublime relations between the persons of the threeness of the oneness that is the Holy Trinity: *paternity*, *filiation*, *spiration*, and *procession*. How unfathomably magnificent it is that the sublime and perfectly simple God is, through his knowledge and love, also the true and perfect family from which earthly families are formed in his image and likeness.

Is God a person — or two or three?

The early sixth-century philosopher Boethius defined a person as "an individual substance of a rational nature."[232] Happily,

---

[230] *ST*, I, Q. 28, art. 1.
[231] Ibid., art. 2.
[232] *ST*, I, Q. 29, art. 1.

according to this definition, both you and I qualify as persons. The only *persons* of all of the creatures on earth are we — individual human beings.[233] The word *person* is not used in the Bible, though. So how is God a person — let alone *three*?

Thomas answers, "*Person* signifies what is most perfect in all nature — that is, a subsistent individual of a rational nature." Hence, since everything that is perfect must be attributed to God, forasmuch as his essence contains every perfection, this name *person* is fittingly applied to God — not, however, as it is applied to creatures, but in a more excellent way."[234] Although the word *person* is not found applied to God in Scripture, what the word *person* means is found many times in Scripture because God is regularly described as "the supreme, self-subsisting and the most perfectly intelligent being."[235] Also, although God's nature is not "rational" in the sense that our rational nature requires that we come to know things through discursive, step-by-step processes, it may be said that God has a rational nature, speaking in the general sense of an intelligent nature.

Thomas notes that to emphasize how the personhood of God exceeds that of creatures, "Richard of St. Victor amends this definition by adding that the *Person* in God is *the incommunicable existence of the divine nature*."[236]

Next, let's take a minute to see what St. Thomas had to communicate about the incommunicable existence of those three divine persons.

---

[233] Note that unborn babies also qualify as persons, for although they are not yet capable of exercising their rational powers, their nature is rational. Rational powers exist in them as potential. This applies to no other species.

[234] ST, I, Q. 29, art. 3.

[235] Ibid.

[236] Ibid.

Who are the Father, the Son, and the Holy Spirit?

God the Father, as St. Augustine says, "is the Principle of the whole Deity," and Thomas adds that "the word principle signifies only that whence another proceeds . . . as the Father then is the one whence another proceeds, it follows is a principle."[237] From the Father proceeds the Son, and from them both, the Holy Spirit. The Father himself proceeds from no principle, but is unbegotten or *innascible*. For human beings, the name *father* describes only a relation of a man to his progeny. In God, the name Father refers not only to a relation, but also to a subsisting person. We also sometimes use the name Father, not as the name of the person, but to refer to the whole Trinity, as when we say, "Our Father" referring to the whole Trinity.

The *Word of God* is a personal name for the *Son of God*, but we must never forget that he is of the same substance as the Father. Those who spoke of the Word of God in only a metaphorical sense gave rise to the Arian heresy, in which the Son was believed to be different from, of a different substance from, and inferior to the Father, thus denying the full divinity of Christ. The Son is also called the *image* of God. Man is made *in* the image of God, while the Son alone *is* the actual image of God.

The *Holy Spirit* shares important things in common with the Father and Son; for example, that they are *spirits* and that they are *holy*. (His name, therefore, is most fitting!) But Thomas also notes that the Holy Spirit can very fittingly be named *Love*, because "the Holy Ghost is said to be the bond of the Father and

---

[237] ST, I, Q. 33, art. 1.

Son, inasmuch as He is Love."[238] The Holy Spirit can also be named *Gift* because as the Son is born of God, the Holy Spirit, in proceeding from Father and Son, is the Gift of God. It is also through the gift of the Holy Spirit that we can partake of God's love.

---

[238] *ST*, I, Q. 37, art. 1. (In a sense, the Father and Son love each other by the Holy Spirit.)

CHAPTER TWENTY-SIX

Why Did God Make the World?

After treating of the procession of the divine persons, we must consider the procession of creatures from God.

—ST, I, Q. 44, prologue

Who created the universe? That is a loaded question, one that could produce a big bang, so to speak. First, it assumes that the universe was created. Some ancient Greek philosophers argued that the universe itself always existed and never was created. You may recall that Thomas presented his five ways to prove God's existence to show that God must exist *even if the universe always existed.* He believed that reason alone could not decide the issue, but *we know the universe was created because God told us so* through the writers of the Scriptures.

Granting through faith that the universe was indeed created in time, the question still raises another question—namely, did God the Father create the universe, or is it the handiwork of the Holy Trinity? Here Thomas tells us, "Dionysius says (*Div. Nom. 2*) that all things caused are the common work of the whole Godhead."[239] God's ability to create belongs to his being

---

[239] *ST*, I, Q. 45, art. 6.

or essence, which is common to the three Persons of the Trinity. God causes things by his intellect and will, as when a craftsman works through an idea or "word" in his mind to craft something that he loves. So too did God the Father make creatures through the Word, who is his Son, and through his Love, which is the Holy Spirit. The Trinity, then, created creation.

So how and why did God do it (create the universe, that is)?

"It must be said that every being in any way existing is from God."[240] We saw in the five ways how no being exists in and of itself except for God. All other beings participate in the being of God. They cannot make themselves to be. Only a being of infinite power can create being *ex nihilo* ("out of nothing"). Matter itself was created by God. When human beings, other creatures, or nature itself, "creates" or "makes" something new, it is always by *changing* something. But that which undergoes change already exists, and God alone produces and sustains existence through a free act of his intellect and will. God alone is the efficient cause, *that by which* the universe was created. God alone is the final cause, too—*that which* all being strives by its nature to return to or to attain. God himself, though, does not act to acquire some end: "He intends only to communicate His perfection, which is His goodness; while every creature intends to *acquire* its own perfection, which is the likeness of divine perfection and goodness. Therefore the divine goodness is the end of all things."[241]

[240] *ST*, I, Q. 44, art. 1.
[241] Ibid., art. 4.

God, then, had no need to create the universe, but did so freely though his love. As Thomas states so eloquently, "He alone is the most perfectly liberal giver, because He does not act for His own profit, but only for His own goodness."[242] Can we take just a minute to let this sink in? Look around you now, remember your past, conjecture about your future. Every single person and thing that is good, true, and beautiful that you have ever seen, and indeed the most wonderful things you have not yet seen and cannot even imagine — all these exist as a free gift from God. What can you do today to show your gratitude to "the most perfectly liberal giver"?

Could anyone else have done it?

Some ancient and medieval thinkers had supposed that God did not create the universe, but it was created by angels. Manicheans supposed it was created by an evil god. Avicenna thought God produced a first intelligence or a separate substance that created another, which in turn produced others that created matter and bodies. Even "the Master" (theologian Peter Lombard) thought that God could delegate to a creature the power of creation, so that it could act instrumentally as his minister, creating through God's power. Thomas argues that God alone possesses the power to create, and one of his simple and interesting arguments is that "it is absurd to suppose that a body can create, for no body acts except by touching or moving; and thus it requires in its action some pre-existing thing, which is to be touched or moved, which is contrary to the very idea of creation."[243]

[242] Ibid.
[243] ST, I, Q. 45, art. 5.

How fascinating and perplexing to think that all of the distinctions and varieties of things in the universe, to the countless varieties of microscopic life to the vastness of galaxies so incredibly far apart, come first from a God who is utterly *simple*. It may help to recall that he is *perfect* as well, the possessor and source of all good to the ultimate degree. Hear Thomas's description for the reason for diversity in creation: "He produced many and diverse creatures, that what was wanting to one in the representation of the divine goodness might be supplied by another. For goodness, which in God is simple and uniform, in creatures is manifold and divided; and hence the whole universe together participates in the divine goodness more perfectly, and represents it better than any simple creature."[244]

Doesn't that explain life's glorious variety? Ants and elephants, football and marbles, male and female . . .

Do you bear the trace and the image of the Trinity?

"Augustine says (*On the Trinity*, 7:10) that "*the trace of the Trinity appears in creatures*."[245] Thomas agrees, recalling that it is the whole Godhead, not just one person of the Trinity, that creates the world. He notes that every effect reflects in some way its cause, but in different ways. Smoke, for example, represents fire, although it is not fire itself. A footprint shows that someone has walked by, although it does not tell us who it was. These imperfect reflections of their causes are present in all created things, "inasmuch as in every creature are found some things which are necessarily reduced to the divine Persons as

[244] *ST*, I, Q. 47, art. 1.
[245] *ST*, I, Q. 45, art. 7.

to their cause."[246] Let's see what he means. (And hang in there, please. We're going to get a bit more abstract than smoke and footprints.)

Every individual creature exists and has its own created substance. This created substance reflects its cause and principle, reflecting the Person of the Father, because he is the uncaused *principle from no principle*. Every creature has a form and species; it is something in particular. This reflects the Person of the Word (the Son), because the form of the thing made by art reflects the word (idea) of the craftsman. The artist determines what his materials will be made into. Finally, every creature has a relationship to other things in the order of the world, which reflects the Holy Spirit, who is love. Love is an act of will, and acts of will establish order.

You and I bear the trace of the Trinity, but we also bear the *image*. An image is more perfectly similar to its cause than is a trace, like smoke. A new fire better represents the fire it started from. A statue of Mercury more clearly represents Mercury. "Therefore in rational creatures, possessing intellect and will, there is found the representation of the Trinity by way of image, inasmuch as there is found in them the word conceived, and the love proceeding."[247]

Why does God permit evil?

The so-called problem of evil leads some away from belief in God. If God is all powerful and all good, why is there pain and evil in the world? Indeed, it is a very good question, and Thomas, as you may have surmised, has some very good

---

[246] Ibid.
[247] Ibid.

answers. First, evil is primarily a *privation*, an *absence of good* where good should be found by a thing's nature. Blindness, for example, is an absence of sight. In a man it is an evil. In a rock it is not. As to the cause of evil, even though it is an absence, Thomas cites Augustine: "*There is no possible source of evil except good.*"[248] Evil is an absence of a good that is natural and due to a thing. Some existing thing must cause that absence, "but only good can be a cause; because nothing can be a cause except inasmuch as it is a being, and every being, as such, is good."[249] Of course, God is the cause of all that is good, and therefore, in one sense, God can be said to be the cause of a certain kind of evil—not directly, but as an indirect effect of the order of the universe and the nature of created beings that can be corrupted and can cease to exist. This is the evil called pain, which can be traced back to God as the first cause, but we must recall, "God is so powerful that He can even make good out of evil."[250]

This is no mere bromide or platitude. Haven't you ever had a bad thing happen to you, and you were surprised later at the greater good that came from it—to point where you're glad the bad thing happened? And note well, God does not *produce* any moral evil in rational creatures, but only *permits* it for greater good. In gracing us with the gift of free will, God leaves open the possibility that we will choose evil things through our own fault. But we can hope and pray that we will choose him instead.

[248] *ST*, I, Q. 49, art. 1.
[249] Ibid.
[250] *ST*, I, Q. 48, art. 3.

Angels: So Smart, They Don't Need to Think!

Next we consider the distinction of corporeal and spiritual creatures: firstly, the purely and spiritual creature which in Holy Scripture is called angel.
—*ST*, I, Q. 50, prologue

There are angels all around us, says Thomas, and lots of them! Indeed, "it must be said that the angels, even inasmuch as they are immaterial substances, exist in exceeding great number, far beyond all material multitude."[251] Recall that it takes the vast multitude of all the creatures in the universe, in their varying degrees of perfection, to reflect imperfectly the simple perfection of God. We have seen that God is spirit, having no body. In questions 50 through 64 of the First Part of the *Summa Theologica*, Thomas uses natural reason and divine revelation to examine the existence and the nature of angels, creatures who reflect the Creator in their immaterial, bodiless, spiritual nature. Inanimate objects, like rocks, have matter but no soul. Vegetables have material bodies and souls, but lack the ability to sense and perceive the world. Animals have bodies and souls

---

[251] *ST*, I, Q. 50, art. 3.

too, along with the ability to know particular things. Human beings also have bodies and souls, but our souls possess *spiritual, intellectual* capacities that allow us to grasp universal principles, to understand things, and to seek what we deem good through the power of free will. Our spiritual intellects and wills, though, must operate on the data that comes from the bodily senses. Angels complete the hierarchy of created beings, possessing yet higher intelligence and will—*without any dependence on a material body.*

Do angels think?

Thomas did not think that angels *ever* think, although they are far more intelligent than any human being. Because we are composite beings of body and soul, our intellectual powers must act upon information brought to us by our senses. We are, as Aristotle called us, rational animals. We have the capacity to reason, that is, to undergo step-by-step processes based on things that we come to know through the mental operations of our intellects acting on information derived from our senses. We use our logical capacities eventually to arrive at new conclusions. The simplest term for such processes is *thinking*, and although no animal but man can do it, "this comes from the feebleness of their [our!] intellectual light."[252]

Angels, having no bodies, are not dependent upon moving step by step from information received by the senses. Their knowledge is not "discursive." It does not involve moving from something previously known to new knowledge that comes after it. Rather, because of the way their powerful intellects are illuminated by God with direct knowledge of the nature of

[252] *ST*, I, Q. 58, art. 3.

things, when they turn their intellects to something, they understand it intuitively — that is, instantly — "as an object and its image are seen simultaneously in a mirror."[253]

How many angels can dance on the head of a pin?

This modern gibe, which pokes fun at medieval theology, cannot be found in the *Summa Theologica*. Although angels have no bodies or measurable quantity, Thomas concluded that they are in only one place at a time — not because they are *contained* by a physical space, but in the sense of *containing it* — as the soul is in the body by containing it, not by being contained by it.

Are Satan and the demons evil?

Perhaps your trick-question alert is going off. Fair enough. Thomas's question is "Whether Any of the Demons Are Naturally Wicked."[254] The key word here is *naturally*, and the answer, in one word, is no! Everything God has created is good in the very fact that it has being. "It is written (Gen. 1:31): *God saw all the things that He made, and they were very good.* But among them were the demons. Therefore the demons were at some time good."[255]

And speaking of very good, the devil himself, by the nature God gave him, was the very highest of the angels. God gave the angels intellects and wills, and those that became evil did so through their own power of choice. And what was the devil's

---

[253] Ibid.
[254] *ST*, I, Q. 63, art. 4.
[255] *ST*, I, Q. 64, art. 5.

evil choice? "It is said, in the person of the devil (Isaiah 14:13-14), *I will ascend into heaven . . . I will be like the Most High.*"[256] Thomas elaborates that the devil's sin of pride consisted in seeking to exist, not as the glorious creature God made him, but as God himself. He sought to attain his own last end of beatitude, not in cooperation with God's grace, but entirely according to his own power, which belongs to God alone and not to even the highest of creatures. He sought as well to be like God in dominion over others. He used his free will to reject God and thereby fell from God's grace and embraced evil, irrevocably rejecting the degree of perfection that was possible to him.

We learn from Revelation 12:4 that "his tail drew the third part of the stars of heaven, and cast them to the earth." The devil did not *cause* a third of the angels to sin and reject God, but he *induced* and exhorted them to make that irrevocable choice of their own free will. They proudly chose him as their prince to lead them to the beatitude they too would obtain without the aid of God.

---

[256] *ST*, I, Q. 63, art. 3.

CHAPTER TWENTY-EIGHT

On the First Day . . . What Happened?

I answer that, In discussing questions of this kind, two rules are to be observed, as Augustine teaches (Gen. ad lit. 1:18). The first is, to hold the truth of Scripture without wavering. The second is that since Holy Scripture can be explained in a multiplicity of senses, one should adhere to a particular explanation, only in such measure as to be ready to abandon it, if it be proved with certainty to be false; lest Holy Scripture be exposed to the ridicule of unbelievers, and obstacles placed to their believing.

—ST, I, Q. 68, art. 1

Did the Bible get things wrong, even "in the beginning"? In our own day, eight centuries after Thomas and seventeen after Augustine, the very first words of the Bible "In the beginning God created heaven, and earth" (Gen. 1:1), and the remainder of the chapter about the works of the six days of Creation, are the subject of ridicule by unbelievers as St. Thomas warned—obstacles to their believing, and instruments used in their efforts to induce unbelief in others. Open a book by a modern atheist, and you will be told that all intelligent, educated, scientifically minded people acknowledge that the universe exists without any need for God and that man was made not by God, but by the chance (and unspecified) workings of evolutionary processes across vast expanses of time. The only alternative belief they present to their own view is that of an antiscientific Bible-thumper who declares that God made the earth in the first six calendar days of the universe six thousand years ago and then took Sunday off.

But even a few minutes spent with St. Thomas will show how false is this modern dichotomy and how steeped in the pursuit of the profound truths of the matter were philosophers and theologians of centuries, indeed, of millennia ago.

Does the Bible show the way the heavens go, or the way to go to heaven?

The seventeenth-century scientist Galileo Galilei once wrote, "The Bible shows the way to go to heaven, not the way the heavens go," relaying a favorite saying of a Vatican librarian of his acquaintance. Unlike modern new atheists and their fundamentalist, Bible-thumping foils, medieval theologians like St. Thomas and the great Greek and Latin Church Fathers from long before his time realized that Scripture is a profound and holy writing with many levels of meaning.[257] Coming from the divine revelation of God himself, the words of the Bible are absolutely true, but our understanding of those words is imperfect, and grows over time through the Holy Spirit's guidance of the Church, and in some ways, through the development of natural, human knowledge as well. St. Thomas stressed mightily

---

[257] Recall from our own chapter 21 St. Thomas's delineation of the *literal* or *historical* sense, along with the *spiritual* sense composed of the *allegorical*, *moral*, and *analogical* senses.

that the truth of faith does not contradict the truth of reason. There is only *one* truth, but there are different means of attaining it.

So, in Thomas's fascinating treatise of "The Work of the Six Days" in questions 65 through 74 of Part I of the *Summa Theologica*, you will find a rich analysis of the meaning of the story of God's creation of the universe, drawing on the profoundest faith, the deepest insights, and the most carefully nuanced reasoning of the greatest thinkers up to his time. In places, the analysis reveals the limited knowledge of science and astronomy at that time. For example, some speculated that the heavenly bodies were alive, or that the extreme coldness of Saturn (the furthest known planet at the time) proved its nearness to the cold waters God had placed above the firmament (Gen. 3:7). On the other hand, St. Thomas was well aware that astronomers said there are many stars larger than the moon—therefore, calling it one of the "two great lights" (Gen. 1:16) does not refer to its size, but to its influence on man and the earth.

Just what is heaven anyway?

One quick example of the careful, nuanced reflection that is required when seeking the meaning of Scripture is shown in Thomas's treatment of the very meaning of the word *heaven* in the Genesis account of God's creation of heaven and earth, and whether there exists more than one heaven: "It is said (Psalm 148:4), *Praise Him, ye heavens of heavens.*"[258] Thomas begins by citing St. John Chrysostom, who said there is only one heaven and the words "heavens of heavens" is a Hebrew idiom in which the word is always shown in plural because it

[258] *ST*, I, Q. 68, art. 4.

has no singular form, just as in Latin there are many such words without a singular form. He then notes that Sts. Basil and John Damascene say that there are many heavens—but that there is no real conflict between the Church Fathers because Scripture uses the word *heaven* in many different senses. Sometimes *heaven* refers to the dwelling place of the blessed, sometimes to the starry firmament, and sometimes to the region between or beyond the stars. At other times still, *heaven* is used metaphorically to refer to God himself, as we see in our day in expressions such as "Heaven help us!"

The need for careful analysis applies to all of the language in the account of creation in Genesis. Indeed, in treating of that first sentence, "In the beginning, God created heaven and earth," not only must we carefully attend to the meaning of *heaven*, but we should note as well that "heaven and earth" encompasses all of creation—"all that is seen and unseen."[259] The words "in the beginning" tell us that *time* itself began with the Creation, contrary to the belief common among Greek thinkers who thought the universe always existed. Further, in stating that *God* created heaven and earth, Moses has shown that God *himself* created all things, contrary to those who thought the angels made man, or as later Manicheans would hold, that the earth was made by an evil god.

Did God really make the world in a week?

Thomas devotes an entire question with articles to each of the seven "days" of creation. Even in the fourth century AD, Christian theologians were careful in their opinions about whether the seven days recounted in Genesis 1 and 2 were

[259] *Catechism of the Catholic Church*, no. 325.

really seven separate calendar days. For example, while most theologians held that the *days* do indicate some kind of succession in time and in the things God produced, Augustine argued that "all the days that are called seven are one day represented in a sevenfold aspect," because he "understands by the word *day*, the knowledge in the mind of the angels . . . which can know many things at the same time, especially in the Word, in Whom all angelic knowledge is perfected and terminated."[260]

The term *day* to Augustine had a deep, symbolic meaning. "Further, it is said (Ecclus. 18:1): *He that liveth for ever, created all things together*."[261] Thomas addresses the conflict in a most interesting way: "God created all things together in terms of their substance in some measure formless. But he did not create all things together, so far as that regards that formation of things which lies in distinction and adornment. Hence the word *creation* is significant."[262] In other words, God produced in potential all that would exist in the first instant of *creation* on the first day at the birth of time itself. In the following periods Moses termed *days*, God's works of *distinction* took place in which he separated light from darkness on day one, the waters from above and under the firmament on day two, and the waters under the heavens from the dry land of the earth on day three. Then followed works of *adornment*, whereby God perfected the heavens on day four, and perfected the earth with creatures of the air and of the sea on day five, and finally with land creatures and man on day six. Whew! What a week! God was then due for a rest.

[260] *ST*, I, Q. 74, art. 2.
[261] Ibid.
[262] Ibid.

If God rested on day seven, where do new species come from?

We'll start by keeping in mind that God as pure act does not get tired and never needs to "rest" in that simple sense of the word! Thomas addresses God's rest on the seventh day in terms of two senses of the word *rest*: "in one sense meaning a cessation from work, in the other, the satisfying of desire."[263] God rested on the seventh day in the first sense, because he stopped making new creatures on that day. In the second sense of rest, God had no need of creatures to satisfy his desires "but was happy in the fruition of Himself. He is not said to have rested in His works, as though needing them for his own happiness, but to have rested from them, as in fact resting in Himself, as He suffices for Himself and fulfils His own desire."[264]

Note well that Genesis 1 tells us that at the end of each day, God saw that his work was "good," and on day six, he saw that everything he made (including man) was "very good" indeed. Although God ceased creating new creatures on the day he "rested," we might call this the most active of all possible rests, for "God indeed *worketh* until now by preserving and providing for the creatures he has made, but not by the making of new ones."[265] And further, God told his creatures to increase and multiply, as continues to this very day.

As for *new* species, God is the first cause of all living beings, but he has given to them secondary powers of causation, not to produce being from nothingness, but to produce changes in

---

[263] *ST*, I, Q. 73, art. 2.
[264] Ibid. God then did not need us, but thank him: he chose to make us!
[265] *ST*, I, Q. 73, art. 2.

190

being that already exist and to reproduce themselves, which may indeed bring changes even in species. Thomas himself notes that new species may appear, for example, when a donkey mates with a mare, producing a mule. If on earth in our day, Thomas would see no inherent contradiction in the Creator's endowing the creatures he produced at the dawn of time with capacity not to create, but to change and evolve over the eons.

Does it make sense to pray?

It sure does. "According to Cassiodorus, *prayer* (oratio) *is spoken reason* (oris ratio)" (*ST*, II-II, Q. 83, art. 1). Speech is a function of the intellect, so prayer is an act not of the sensitive powers, but of the intellectual powers, and it's uniquely human.

Lower animals cannot pray. When Psalm 146:9 tells us that God gives food to the beasts and ravens that call upon him, it refers to the natural, instinctual desire for God implanted in animals, and not to actual prayer.

God himself does not pray because there is nothing he needs from another. Further, prayer is an act of reason that consists in beseeching or requesting things from a superior. No being is above the Divine Persons of God.

Prayer, then, is the province of the rational animal, and that animal is man. Thomas notes that prayer starts with and is essentially *"the raising up of one's mind to God"* (*ST*, II-II, Q. 83, art. 17) and that the "parts" of prayer include *supplications* (humble requests) for particular blessings from God and *thanksgivings* for blessings he has already provided.

CHAPTER TWENTY-NINE

God Rules . . . Every Single Thing!

It would seem that the world is not governed by anyone . . . On the contrary, it is written (Wis. 14:3): But Thou, O Father, governest all things by Thy Providence. And Boethius says (De Consol. 3): Though Who governest this universe by mandate eternal.

—*ST*, Q. 103, art. 1

A human governor executes the laws of a state, hopefully for the good of the state and of the individuals it comprises. God executes his eternal laws for the benefit of the creatures of all the universe in a way that immeasurably exceeds the scope and power of any human ruler, for the good he leads us to is himself, and he governs us not only in the sense of guiding our actions, but in the sense of sustaining our very existence.

As Thomas notes, "Even that which is stable, since it is created from nothing, would return to nothingness were it not sustained by a governing hand."[266] The *order* and *purpose* we see in the actions of created things refute the belief of some ancient

---

[266] *ST*, I, Q. 103, art. 1.

(and modern) philosophers that everything happens by *chance*. The very fact that created beings *exist* puts the lie to the idea that God created the world, but takes no active role in it now: "Foolish therefore was the opinion of those who said that the corruptible lower world, or individual things, or that even human affairs, were not subject to the Divine government. These are represented as saying, *God hath abandoned the earth* (Ezech. 9:9)."[267] This is an astounding fact to consider. God's action *sustains* our very existence, preventing all that he created from returning to nothingness. Thomas says, "Every creature may be compared to God, as the air is to the sun which enlightens it."[268] Without the light of the sun, the air becomes instantly dark.

Does God govern everything directly?

God's providence governs everything, but not immediately or directly. "In government there are two things to be considered; the design of government, which is providence itself; and the execution of the design. As to the design of government, God governs all things immediately; whereas in its execution, He governs some things by means of others."[269] Government's role is to bring to perfection the things that are governed. "Now it is a greater perfection for a thing to be good in itself and also the cause of goodness in others, than only to be good in itself. Therefore God so governs things that He makes some of them to be causes of others in government; as a master, who not only imparts knowledge to his pupils, but gives also the faculty of teaching others."[270]

[267] *ST*, I, Q. 103, art. 5.
[268] *ST*, I, Q. 104, art. 1.
[269] *ST*, I, Q. 103, art. 6.
[270] Ibid.

Let's pause and reflect a bit on the gloriously generous way that God governs creation. He is the immediate and direct cause of all creatures, having created them and preserving them in existence "by continually pouring out existence to them."[271] Not only does he give us, made in his image and likeness, our existence and our capacity to seek him as our final perfection, but he grants us secondary powers, through the gift of intellect and free will, to govern ourselves and to help bring our neighbors to their own perfection. The role of the teacher is the perfect example to illustrate this governing power bestowed upon us — to "pay it forward," so to speak, in sharing God's light with others, so that they, when enlightened, may enlighten others. Further, as the dignity of an earthly kind is evidenced by the power he assigns to his hierarchy of ministers, so too is God's dignity revealed by the authority he generously delegates to us.

There is order and hierarchy even among the angels.[272]

Why do some modern thinkers think there is a problem with angels?

Some modern thinkers have little sense of what an angel is. Many people know that the word *angel* itself means "messenger." Angels of all the orders, in some sense, carry forth the messages of God. But just what are these messengers? Many may think of them in their popular, sentimental, artistic renderings, like the chubby little cherubim babies, and they doubt that such beings really exist. Others, who are aware of St. Thomas's description

---

[271] *ST*, I, Q. 104, art. 4.

[272] In one of the most speculative sections of the *Summa Theologica*, in question 108, building on the writings of Scripture, Dionysius, and St. Gregory the Great, he provides this fascinating summary.

Order and Hierarchy of Angels

Highest Orders
They contemplate the idea of things in God himself
and have the closest relation to Him.

Seraphim   They are most closely united to God, singing perpetual praises around his throne.

Cherubim   They know the Divine secrets "supereminently" through God himself.

Thrones   They receive judgments from God and pass them on to the second hierarchy.

Middle Orders
They contemplate the idea of things in
universal causes and are involved in governing.

Dominations   They appoint things that are to be done.

Virtues   They carry out what is to be done.

Powers   They decide how what has been commanded will be carried out by others.

Lowest Orders
They contemplate the idea of things in their application
to particular effects and they execute God's works.

Principalities   They act as rulers, presiding over the government of peoples and kingdoms of the earth.

Archangels   They announce to men great things above the power of reason.

Angels   They announce to men small things within the limits of reason.

of angels as purely spiritual beings (as we saw in chapter 27), believe that the idea of an *immaterial intelligence* is a contradiction in terms, much like a round square. These are *materialists* who believe it impossible for something to be or exist without having a body. Ironically, they are using the immaterial, conceptual powers of their intellectual souls to deny that any existing thing can truly be immaterial. In this form of denial, to be consistent, they must deny God as well.

We have but a minute here, of course. But for those intrigued by the subject of angels as another manifestation of the wondrously ordered universe God created, please seek out Part I of the *Summa Theologica* itself, questions 50 through 64 and 106 through 114. They are full of fascinating insights on topics ranging from the ways in which angels communicate with each other to the existence of guardian angels to the nature, history, and powers of the fallen angels.

If you would find intriguing a modern philosophical analysis of the possibility of the existence of angels *based on reason alone*, written by a philosopher highly influenced by St. Thomas Aquinas, who called himself a pagan at the time he wrote his book on angels, and yet who died nineteen years later as a member of the Catholic Church, I respectfully direct you to Mortimer J. Adler's *The Angels and Us*.

PART III

Who Is Christ?

Being born, He became our friend.
At supper, He became our food.
Dying, He was our ransom's price.
And, reigning, is our eternal good.

—St. Thomas Aquinas, "The Word
from Heaven Now Proceeding"[273]

---

[273] This is a the fourth stanza of St. Thomas's prayer *Verbum Supernum Prodiens*, "The Word from Heaven Now Proceeding," as it appears in R. Anderson and J. Moser, trans. and eds., *The Aquinas Prayer Book: The Prayers and Hymns of St. Thomas Aquinas* (Manchester, NH: Sophia Institute Press, 2000), 97.

CHAPTER THIRTY

Why Did God Become Man?

---

*After considering the last end of human life,
and the virtues and vices, there should follow
the consideration of the Savior of all, and of the
benefits bestowed by Him on the human race.*

—ST, III, prologue

We started with the material on man in Part II of the *Summa* as
kind of a mental warm-up before covering the material on God
in Part I, like wading into shallow waters before immersing ourselves in the depths of God's mysteries that even the highest of
seraphim cannot completely tread. Well, we hope we've stayed
afloat and managed to fathom them to some extent, for now it
is time to sail into Part III, to see how God's waters of goodness
overflowed in the great flood of grace that brought him to the
earth *as a man*, so that we, through his grace, might one day
dwell in heaven with him.[274]

---

[274] If you'll pardon a personal note, I can't help observing that
this was also the sequence of parts of the *Summa Theologica*,
through which I, in my mid-forties, found myself drawn back
into the doors of the Church after twenty-five years in the
atheistic wilderness. As a psychologist specializing in memory,

Stay tuned then, as we take a few minutes to look at the In-carnation, the role of the Blessed Virgin Mary, the life of Christ, and the Church and the sacraments he established on earth so that we might live in eternal bliss with him, as God's adopted sons and daughters.

How did God become man?

Now there is a question that not even St. Thomas can an-swer in full. The *Incarnation* is one of the great *mysteries* of the faith, exceeding human understanding. Yet it is reasonable to believe it, because we know that God's power is limitless. As Augustine has written, "God is great not in mass, but in might. Hence the greatness of His might feels no straits in narrow sur-roundings. Nor, if the passing word of man is heard at once

---

I respected Thomas's role in the development and endorse-ment of memory technique (including *ST*, II-II, Q. 49, art. 1), which drew me to the rest of Part II. Impressed by his amaz-ingly accurate and thorough portrayal of the nature of man, I was led to writings on God in Part I, which showed me the awesome splendor of God and the reasonableness of belief in the God of the Five Ways. Thomas showed as well that this "god of the philosophers" was also the "God of Abraham, Isaac, and Jacob," the God of the Old Testament, who is also the God of the New Testament. Seeking a way to worship and unite with the will of the Triune God described in Part I led to my immersion in Part III, relishing again the knowl-edge of Jesus Christ and seeking to renew a relationship with him through the earthly instrument he established for that purpose, the same Roman Catholic Church into which I had been baptized in my first months of life. So, although it took me twenty-five years, regaining my faith, with the grace of God and the *Summa Theologica*, was as easy as II, I, III!

by many, and wholly by each, is it incredible that the abiding Word of God should be everywhere at once?"[275]

We can believe in faith with absolute certainty that the Eternal Word of God entered time and became man because God himself has revealed it on earth in the person of Jesus Christ. His story is told in the Scriptures, prefigured in the Old Testament, and fulfilled in the New.

God made man
"that man might be made God"

This is a most crucial issue, if not the most crucial of all. God became incarnate as the most fitting way to restore our corrupted sinful human nature so that many good things would follow, including the building up of our *faith*, since we could hear God Himself speak; our *hope*, since Christ's presence shows us God's love for us; our *charity*, so that we would desire to love God in return for his presence among us; and our *well-doing*, since God himself served as our example; and indeed, "the full participation of the Divinity, which is the bliss of man and end of human life; and this is bestowed on us by Christ's humanity; for Augustine says in a sermon (8, *de Temp.*): *God was made man, that man might be made God*."[276]

Such a gift is the Incarnation that of the sin of Adam that led to the corruption of our human nature, we say in the blessing of the Paschal candle: *O happy fault, that merited such, and so great a Redeemer!*[277]

[275] *ST*, III, Q. 1, art. 1.
[276] Ibid., art. 2.
[277] Ibid., art. 3.

Could the Father or Holy Spirit have taken on human flesh?

Sure. Thomas says, "Whatever the Son can do, so can the Father and the Holy Ghost, otherwise the power of the three Persons would not be one. But the Son was able to become incarnate. Therefore, the Father and the Holy Ghost were able to become incarnate."[278] It was, however, most fitting for the Person of the Son to do so, indeed, for several fascinating reasons!

First, as the "word" or concept in the mind of a wise craftsman is the "exemplar likeness" or as the mental prototype gives rise to whatever he makes, so too "the Word of God, Who is His eternal concept, is the exemplar likeness of all creatures."[279] (Recall that we profess of the Son in the Nicene Creed, "Through him all things were *made*.") So too, as the "word" of the craftsman restores a handiwork that gets damaged, it is fitting that the Word of God should *restore* our damaged human nature.

Secondly, the incarnation of the Son is fitting because the Incarnation fulfills the predestination of God. Heavenly inheritance is bestowed upon God's sons "according to Rom. 8:17; *If sons, heirs also.* Hence it was fitting that by Him Who is the natural Son, men should share his likeness of sonship by adoption, as the apostle says in the same chapter (8:29) *For whom He foreknew, he also predestined to be made conformable to the image of His Son.*"[280]

Third, Christ's incarnation remedies the sin of our first parent, Adam, who sought knowledge of good and evil. How fitting "that by the Word of true knowledge man might be led

---

[278] ST, III, Q. 3, art. 5.
[279] Ibid., art. 8.
[280] Ibid.

back to God, having wandered from God through an inordinate thirst for knowledge."[281]

Although our minds cannot grasp in full the nature of Christ's Incarnation, it makes such glorious sense that the heavenly Son of Man would right the wrongs of man's earthly father.

How can Jesus Christ be one person with two natures and one will?

This question cleaved apart parts of the early Church. Thomas recounts how the wrong answers led to various heresies, such as Nestorius's position proclaiming that within Jesus were two persons, one divine and one human and that Mary was not the Mother of God but only the mother of Christ's humanity. Although these issues are conceptually difficult and I just have a minute to scratch their surfaces here, let me note that our Catholic faith holds that Jesus Christ is one person with two natures and one will. A *nature* signifies the essence, quiddity, or the "whatness" of something. In the Incarnation, the Son of God assumed, in addition to his divine nature as God, a human nature, complete in body and soul. He acquired all the bodily and intellectual powers and defects of humanity for our sake, yet without any loss of his divine nature or split in his personhood. Therefore, what Christ became was God *and* man.

Now, a person, per Boethius, "is nothing else than an individual substance of rational nature."[282] A human person is an individual who has a human nature, and in Jesus Christ, the person of the Word assumed an *individual* human nature, not human nature in general; otherwise, every man would be the

[281] Ibid.
[282] *ST*, III, Q. 2, art. 2.

Word of God. Christ, then, is one person (the Son of God) with two natures (divine and human), with one intellect and will that partake in both his divine and human natures.

Was Jesus lacking in faith and hope?

Jesus possessed in full all of the virtues and gifts, except for faith and hope. Thomas makes quite clear, though, that this was no lack or deficiency. We read in Hebrews 11:1: "Now faith is the substance of things to be hoped for, the evidence of things that appear not" and as is said of Christ in John 21:17: "Lord, though knowest all things." Faith and hope pertain to things unseen. Jesus didn't need them, because he already saw all.[283]

Who is the head of the Church?

Christ received the fullness of God's grace, not only as an individual, but as the Head of the Church, his Mystical Body, of which we are the members. "He has the power of bestowing grace on all the members of the Church, according to John 1:16: *Of His fullness we have all received.* And thus it is plain that Christ is fittingly called the Head of the Church."[284] Christ serves as the head by directing our actions interiorly through grace, as our head guides our bodily movements. Further, as the head also uses "a certain exterior guidance, inasmuch as by sight and the senses, which are rooted in the head,"[285] other members of the church, such as bishops, act as heads in their dioceses, and the Pope acts as head of the whole Church, providing exterior guidance to the mystical body through the authority of Christ.

---

[283] *ST*, III, Q. 7, arts. 3, 4. As we saw in chapter 7, neither will we need them when we see God face-to-face.

[284] *ST*, III, Q. 8, art. 2.

[285] Ibid., art. 7.

In what way can we say that Jesus is the way?

Jesus is the perfect mediator between God and man and the only way to our salvation. "It is written (1 Tim. 2:5); *There is one Mediator of God and man, the man Christ Jesus.*" Thomas tells us that the role of "a mediator is to join together and unite those between whom he mediates; for extremes are united in the mean (*medio*)."[286] Pope Leo once elaborated in a sermon on Christ as Mediator: "Unless He was God, He would not have brought a remedy; and unless He was man, He would not have set an example."[287] Jesus cleared the way for us to eternal bliss, and he came down to show us that way. He himself set the perfect example in his life, death, and Resurrection, as we'll examine in the next two chapters. He established, as part of the remedy, a holy Church on earth to administer his sacraments to help us all achieve heaven. We'll examine these in a few minutes.

[286] *ST*, III, Q. 26, art. 2.
[287] *ST*, III, Q. 1, art. 2.

CHAPTER THIRTY-ONE

Hail, Full of Grace!

---

*For it is reasonable to believe that she, who brought
forth the Only-Begotten of the Father, full of grace
and truth, received greater privileges of grace than
all others; hence we read (Luke 1:28) that the angel
addressed her in the words: Hail, full of grace!*

—ST, III, Q. 27, art. 1

Are Thomas's writings about the Blessed Virgin Mary relevant today?

Absolutely! St. Thomas's wrote about Blessed Mary in the
thirteenth century, answering heretical opinions from many
centuries before that. Still, his writings remain relevant to any
modern Christian who would care to know how to venerate
the blessed woman who served as God's instrument in the Holy
Incarnation that would redeem the human race. And indeed, in
our day there are many misconceptions among Christians about
the respect and love that is properly due to Holy Mary. Some
non-Catholics argue that Catholics worship Mary as a goddess,
and they deny the four *de fide* ("by faith") Marian dogmas of
the Catholic Church: that she is the *Mother of God*, her *perpetual virginity*, her *Immaculate Conception*, and her *assumption into
Heaven*. Some even misrepresent St. Thomas's own position on

de fide Marian doctrines.[288] Within the *Summa Theologica*, St. Thomas deftly explains and defends two of those dogmas, affirms another in passing, and indeed, argues against one.[289] Let's dig in, then, to revel in the truths of the Angelic Doctor and to examine carefully one of his rare mistakes.

Did Blessed Mary remain perpetually virgin?

This was a question recently on my own mind as I wrote a chapter on the dogma of Mary's perpetual virginity in my most recent book defending core beliefs of the Catholic Faith.[290] The Catholic Church tells us the answer is an unequivocal *yes!* (So did the earliest Protestant reformers, such as Luther, Calvin, and Zwingli.) Yet, in our day, many Protestant Christians will agree that Christ was born of the virgin Mary, but will protest that she did not remain a virgin after Christ's birth, noting, for example, that Scripture tells us Joseph did not "know" Mary *until* she had borne Jesus (Matt. 1:25), that Christ had been called

---

[288] Indeed I came across today an interview with an Evangelical theologian who made this statement: "Aquinas never believed in the bodily assumption of Mary, which was defined in 1950" ("Thomas Aquinas: Christian History Interview—He's Our Man," interview with Norman Geisler, *Christianity Today*, January 1, 2002, http://www.ctlibrary.com/ch/2002/issue73/13.43.html, accessed August 10, 2013). We'll examine this further in just a minute.

[289] Note that it had not yet been defined by the Pope and the Magisterium of the Church. Theologians were free to weigh in on both sides of the issue at that time. We'll examine this too in another minute!

[290] *Memorize the Reasons!* (San Diego: Catholic Answers Press, 2013), chap. 6.

firstborn, perhaps implying other children (Matt. 1:25; Rom. 8:29), and that Jesus was said to have *brethren* (John 2:12).

In reading the four articles of St. Thomas's question 28 of Part III, "Of the Virginity of the Mother of God," we get a glimpse of how old these and other arguments against Blessed Mary's perpetual virginity are and of how long ago they were so soundly refuted![291] Thomas notes, for example, citing Jerome, that "Scripture speaks of brethren in four senses: namely, those who are united by being of the same parents, of the same nation, of the same family, by common affection."[292] Thomas also explains how Mary had taken a vow of perpetual virginity to God before the Annunciation, since she asked the angel Gabriel how she could bear a child without knowing man, even though she was espoused to Joseph. Further, Thomas notes that by being a perpetual virgin, but also a married woman and a mother, "both virginity and wedlock are honored in her person, in contradiction to those heretics who disparaged one or the other."[293]

Should the Blessed Virgin be called the Mother of God?

This is the question Thomas asked in article 4 of question 35 in Part III of the *Summa*. Early heresies had arisen because some argued that Mary gave birth only to Christ's human nature and not his divine nature. Thomas echoed the Council at

[291] One of St. Thomas's main sources for his arguments come from St. Jerome's answers to one Helvidius, who argued that Mary had other children after Jesus. St. Jerome's work, *Against Helvidius*, was written in 383 AD.

[292] *ST*, III, Q. 28, art. 3.

[293] *ST*, III, Q. 29, art. 1.

Ephesus, which declared as dogma that "*the Holy Virgin is the Mother of God.*"[294] Human mothers give birth not to natures, but to persons. Likewise, Mary gave birth not to a nature, but to a Person, the Person of Christ, who possessed both divine and human natures. Thomas notes, "We do not find it in the Scripture that the Blessed Virgin is the Mother of God, yet we do find it expressly said in Scripture that *Jesus Christ is true God*, as may be seen in 1 John 5:20, and that the Blessed Virgin is the *Mother of Jesus Christ*, which is clearly expressed in Matt: 1:18. Therefore, from the words of Scripture it follows of necessity that she is the Mother of God."[295]

Was Mary assumed into heaven, body and soul?

As I noted just a couple of minutes ago, it has been inaccurately stated that Thomas did not believe in Holy Mary's bodily assumption, which was defined in 1950. Well, it is true that Thomas did not address the Assumption in an article or question of its own. Still, when Pope Pius XII promulgated the dogma on November 1, 1950, he stated: "Following the footsteps of his distinguished teacher, the Angelic Doctor, despite the fact that he never dealt directly with this question, nevertheless, whenever he touched upon it, always held, together with the Catholic Church, that Mary's body had been assumed into heaven along with her soul."[296]

[294] *ST*, III, Q. 35, art. 1.
[295] Ibid.
[296] Pius XII, Apostolic Constitution *Munificentissimus Deus*, defining the Dogma of the Assumption, http://www.vatican.va/holy_father/pius_xii/apost_constitutions/documents/hf_p-xii_apc_19501101_munificentissimus-deus_en.html.

Was Mary conceived without sin?

Although he believed that Mary was sinless, Thomas answered this question *no*, and the Holy Church declared clearly later that the true answer is a resounding *yes!*[297] The English Dominican Fathers who edited the *Summa Theologica* note that Thomas reasoned that the Blessed Virgin was not sanctified before "animation" (the joining of the soul with the body at conception). "Such a conclusion would hold if it were a question of the order of Nature: a thing must be before it is such (*prius est esse quamesse tale*); and therefore the soul must be, before it is sanctified. But if Thomas held for a posteriority of time, no matter how short, we ask how it was that he did not perceive the fallacy of the argument, since it might be neither before nor after, but in the very instant of animation."[298]

They note further that the issue had not yet been defined by the Church. Learned theologians had opinions on either side of the issue. Thomas was among those, including Sts. Bernard, Albert the Great, and Bonaventure, who believed that Mary was sanctified *in the womb*. Later, thinkers including Duns Scotus in the early fourteenth century would build upon the

---

The Angelic Doctor's "distinguished teacher" was St. Albert the Great, who wrote eloquently about the Assumption. Pope Pius XII noted that passages from the *Summa Theologica* in which St. Thomas mentions the Assumption include question 27, article 1, and question 83, article 5 in Part III. In question 27, Thomas cites with approval Augustine's tractate on the *Assumption of the Virgin*, and in question 83, he does the same from a decretal of Pope Sergius mentioning Mary, with her body, in glory in heaven with Christ.

[297] On December 8, 1854, in Pope Pius IX's *Ineffabilis Deus*.

[298] Fathers of the English Dominican Province, trans., *Summa Theologica* (NY: Benzinger, 1948), 2155.

foundation laid by Thomas and others and resolve the difficulties. Thomas argued that the Mother of God was *redeemed* by Christ, as are all men, and the grace of her sanctification *preserved* her from sin. These doctrines would serve as the basis for Scotus's solution showing that Mary's redemption was not only one of *preservation* in her sinless state, but also one of *prevention* of even Original Sin from the very instant of her conception. To use a simple analogy, Christ redeems us by pulling us out after we fall into deep holes of sin. Christ redeemed his Holy Mother by preventing even one step toward the edge. God so greatly honored the human Mother of his Son; no wonder we all should most truly hail Mary!

CHAPTER THIRTY-TWO

Christ's Life, and What Made It Perfect

In his manner of living our Lord gave an example of perfection as to all those things which of themselves relate to salvation.

—ST, III, Q. 40, art. 2

At the end of his Gospel, St. John the evangelist wrote that Jesus did so many other things, "if they were written every one, the world itself, I think, would not be able to contain the books that should be written" (John 21:25). Now, the world certainly has plenty of room to contain all that St. Thomas wrote about Jesus, but, alas, *The One-Minute Aquinas* can hold but the slightest fraction of the Angelic Doctor's insights on Christ as the Word of God, the *Alpha* and the *Omega*,[299] Priest, Prophet, King, Lawgiver, Judge, and Savior, in his conception, birth, circumcision, manner of life, temptation, teaching, miracles, transfiguration, passion, death, descent into hell, Resurrection, Ascension into heaven, and in his place at the right hand of the Father.

---

[299] "I am Alpha and Omega, the first and the last, the beginning and the end" (Rev. 22:13).

In the questions ahead, we will get a brief glimpse of a few of the great themes focusing on Christ's manner of life, teaching, Passion, death, and Resurrection but will also sample smaller, yet intriguing issues to give some sense of the seriousness with which St. Thomas and the great Greek and Latin Church Fathers considered the seemingly smallest of details of the life of Christ. Indeed, the 29 questions on Christ following the questions on Blessed Mary include 158 articles addressing many aspects of the perfect way that Christ's Incarnation led to the Redemption of mankind and to sublime lessons to be learned for our lives on earth.

Should the matter of Christ's body have come only from a woman?

That the matter of Christ's body came only from a woman is clearly stated in Scripture. "It is written (Gal. 4:4): *God sent His Son, made of a woman.*"[300] In addressing how fitting it is that God made this so, Thomas provides some thought-provoking answers, including the following: God accomplishes the begetting of man "in every variety of manner." God made the first man "from the *slime of the earth*" without a man or woman, Eve was made from a man without a woman, other men and women are made from both man and woman, "so that this fourth manner remained as it were proper to Christ, that he should be made of a woman without the occurrence of a man."[301] That Christ came as a man and was born of a woman does honor to both sexes.

[300] *ST*, III, Q. 31, art. 4.
[301] Ibid.

Should Christ's birth have been made known by angels and a star?

Yes: "It is written (Deut. 32:4), *The works of God are perfect*."[302] The Jewish people were used to receiving divine messages from angels, as we see in Acts 7:53, when St. Paul told them they had "received the law by the disposition of the angels." So, it was fitting that an angel informed the shepherds of the birth of their Lord and Savior. Since the Gentiles in general, and astrologers in particular, observed the course of the stars, it was fitting that the three Magi were led to the Christ child by the star over Bethlehem.

Chrysostom also said that some questionable books told of a tribe in the Far East possessing a book by Seth that referred to a star containing the figure of a small child and a cross. Augustine speculated that the Magi were given a special revelation by angels that the star signified the birth of Christ. Pope Leo wrote that beside the physical light of the star, a more brilliant spiritual ray enlightened the Magi's minds with the light of faith.

Why did Christ hang out with people?

Christ lived the kind of life he did to fulfill the three main ends of his Incarnation, the very reasons he came into the world. First, he came to proclaim the truth: "thus He says Himself (John 18:37): *For this I was born, and for this I came into the world, that I should give testimony to the truth.*" For that reason, he lived a social, public life, interacting with and preaching to others.

---

[302] *ST*, III, Q. 36, art. 5.

Secondly, Christ came to free us from sin: "According to 1 Tim. 1:35: *Christ Jesus came into the world to save sinners.*"[303] Therefore, Christ did not live a solitary, stationary life, but as Chrysostom notes, Christ went out in search of sinners like a shepherd searching for lost sheep or a physician making his rounds.

"Thirdly, He came that we might have access to God, as it is written (Rom 5:2). And thus it was fitting that He should give men and women confidence in approaching Him by associating familiarly with them."[304] Christ then, clearly sought us out, in hopes that we would do the same and seek him out. It should boggle the mind that the Word through whom all things were made wants us to feel familiar with him. Perhaps we should ask ourselves, then, to what extent we have taken him up on this most generous of all offers.

Why wasn't Christ an author?

Clearly, he had more important things to do! Thomas noted that Christ did not commit his doctrine to writing because of his excellence and dignity. *He taught by his life* so that his lessons became *engraved on his hearers' hearts.*[305] Further, his doctrine was so excellent, it could not be expressed fully in words. Finally, he intended his message to be spread by others (such as the evangelists, the Church Fathers, and twelve hundred years later, by St. Thomas Aquinas).

---

[303] *ST*, III, Q. 40, art. 1.

[304] Ibid.

[305] *ST*, III, Q. 43, art. 4. Thomas notes that among the Gentiles, most excellent teachers such as Pythagorus and Socrates did not write anything on paper either.

Why did Christ suffer temptation by the devil?

"Christ wished to be tempted first so that He might *strengthen us* against temptations."[306]

Christ intended to *warn us* so that nobody should think he is so holy that he cannot be tempted.

Christ *supplied us an example* to teach us how to overcome the temptations of the devil.

Christ was tempted "in order to *fill us with confidence in his mercy.* Hence it is written (Heb. 4:15): *We have not a high-priest, who cannot have compassion on our infirmities, but one tempted in all things like as we are, without sin.*"[307]

What can we learn about Christ from his miracles?

"Christ worked miracles in order to confirm His doctrine and in order to show forth his Divine Power."[308] These are the two reasons God works miracles: that is, to confirm doctrines of faith that exceed human reason and cannot be proven by arguments, and to show that the man who performs the miracles does so by the grace and power of God. Christ did not perform miracles until he reached the perfect age to begin to teach, and he did not want to manifest his divine power in his early years, *"for men would have deemed the Incarnation to be imaginary and would have crucified Him before his proper time."*[309] Christ's miracles proved his Godhead because they surpassed what any

[306] *ST*, III, Q. 41, art. 1.
[307] Ibid.
[308] *ST*, III, Q. 43, art. 3.
[309] Ibid.; citing St. John Chrysostom's *Homily on John's Gospel.*

created power could do; because he worked them through his own power, and not through prayer, as others do; and because he taught he was God. If this were not true, it would not be confirmed by miracles of Divine Power.

Was there a better way to heal us than by Christ's Passion?

"St. Augustine says (*On the Trinity*, 8): There was no other more suitable way of healing our misery than by the Passion of Christ."[310]

Christ's Passion did many other things besides delivering us from sin:

• It shows man how much God loves us, stirs us to return that love which perfects our human salvation (see Rom. 5:8).

• It sets for us "an example of obedience, humility, constancy, justice, and the other virtues displayed in the Passion, which are requisite for man's salvation"[311] (see 1 Pet. 2:21).

• It merited justice and grace for man and the glory of bliss (see Phil. 2:9).

• It binds man all the more to refrain from sin because we were bought with such a great price (see 1 Cor. 6:20).

• "It redounded to man's greater dignity, that as man was overcome and deceived by the devil, so also it should

---

[310] *ST*, III, Q. 46, art. 4.
[311] Ibid.

be a man that should overthrow the devil; and as man deserved death, so a man by dying should vanquish death"[312] (see 1 Cor. 15:5).

• By Christ's Passion we were delivered from sin, reconciled to God, delivered from the devil's power, freed from the punishment of sin, and "the gates of heaven's kingdom"[313] were thrown open to us. Christ himself also received a fourfold exaltation through his passion in the form of 1) his glorious Resurrection, 2) his Ascension into heaven, 3) his sitting at the right hand of the Father, showing forth his Godhead, and 4) his power of judgment over the living and dead.

What does Jesus Christ's Resurrection mean for you and me?

"It is written (Luke 24:46): *It behooved Christ to rise again from the dead.*"[314] Thomas then gives five reasons why (and why it behooves us, too).

• It commends Divine Justice, which exalts those who humble themselves for God's sake (see Luke 1:52; Ps. 138:2).

• It instructs us in our faith, for "it is written (1 Cor. 15:14): *If Christ not be risen again, then is our preaching vain, and our* [Vulgate—*your*] *faith is also vain* (see also 2 Cor. 8:4).

[312] Ibid.
[313] *ST*, III, Q. 49, art. 5.
[314] *ST*, III, Q. 53, art. 1.

- It raises our hope, because when we see Christ — the mystical head of the Church — rise again, we hope that we too shall rise (see 1 Cor. 15:12; Job 18:25-27).

- It sets "in order the lives of the faithful: according to Rom. 6:4: *As Christ is risen from the dead by the glory of the Father, so we may also walk in newness in life;* and further on: *Christ rising from the dead, dieth now no more; so do you also reckon that you are dead to sin, but alive to God.*"[315]

- It completes the work of our salvation. Christ endured evil things in dying to deliver us from evil, "so He was gloried in rising again in order to advance us toward good things; according to Rom. 4:25; *He was delivered up for our sins, and rose again for our justification.*"[316]

[315] *ST*, III, Q. 53, art. 1.
[316] Ibid.

DUMB OX BOX #9
Should we pray for ourselves — or for others?

Yes. That is, both. As for ourselves, Thomas notes that it is proper and fitting to pray for even temporal, earthly goods for ourselves. Proverbs 30:8 is an example of praying for the basic necessities of life. And of course, in the Lord's Prayer we ask for our "daily bread."

Problems arise when worldly things become our main focus and goal, serving as ends rather than means of acquiring the highest beatitude that comes from joining with God.

As for praying for others, "It is written (James 5:16): *Pray for one another, that you may be saved.*" Indeed, "charity requires us to pray for others" as an expression of our love of neighbor. Further, "as Cyprian says (*De Orat. Dom.*), *We say, 'Our Father' and not 'My Father'; 'Give us' and not 'Give me' . . . The Master of unity did not wish us to pray privately, that is, for ourselves alone, for He wished each one to pray for all, even as He Himself bore all in one.*'" (*ST*, II-II, Q. 83, art. 7).

Ancient Irish Christians spoke disapprovingly of *phaidir ghann*, a "scarce prayer," or "stingy prayer," in which one prayed only for oneself.

One of Thomas's early teachers was a man called Peter of Ireland. Surely Thomas learned this lesson well, and he stands ready now in heaven to intercede for us with his prayers.

CHAPTER THIRTY-THREE

Sacraments: The Seven Holy Signs of God

After considering those things that concern the mystery of the incarnate Word, we must consider the sacraments of the Church which derive their efficacy from the Word incarnate Himself.

—*ST*, III, Q. 60, prologue

What do we mean by *sacrament*?

A sacrament is a *"sign of a holy thing so far as it makes men holy."*[317] Signs are sensible, familiar things that point to things other the signs themselves. It is part of human nature to acquire knowledge of higher things through the information that comes from our senses. In the sacraments of the Church, visible, material things such as water, oil, bread, and wine point to invisible, but real and powerful graces poured into us by God. Those graces serve to perfect our holiness in a variety of ways particular to each of the Church's sacraments.

Sacraments are also means of worshipping God. In addition to sensible, material *signs*, sacraments employ *words* as signs of our sanctification. This is most appropriate for several reasons.

[317] *ST*, III, Q. 60, art. 2.

First, the sacraments use words that speak of the cause of our sanctification—which is the Word Incarnate. In this way, the sacraments bear resemblance to Christ, who initiated them. Sacraments join words to material signs, as in the Incarnation—wherein the Word was joined to sensible flesh.

Secondly, as men who are sanctified by the sacraments are composed of soul and body, the sacraments touch the body through the material elements and the soul through faith in the words.

Third, words are the primary means by which we express ideas with greatest clarity. For example, "when we say, *I baptize thee*, it is clear we use water in order to signify a spiritual cleansing"[318] rather than merely to cleanse or to cool the body.

Why do we need sacraments when Christ died for our salvation?

Some argued in Thomas's day and before (and some still do!) that we do not need the Church's sacraments because, for example, "the Apostle says (1 Tim. 4:8): Bodily exercise is profitable to little,"[319] in contrast to spiritual exercise, and sacraments are like physical exercises because they employ sensible things. Further, Christ told St. Paul, "My grace is sufficient for you" (2 Cor. 12:9, RSV), so sacraments aren't needed since Christ's grace suffices. Further, when a cause is sufficient to produce an effect, nothing else is needed. We are told in Romans 5:10 that we were reconciled to God by Christ's death and saved by his life. Christ died and rose to achieve our salvation. Why on earth (or in heaven) would we need sacraments?

[318] *ST*, III, Q. 60, art. 6.
[319] *ST*, III, Q. 61, art. 1.

Thomas answers that for salvation, humanity must be united in the one true religion, and as Augustine has noted, one cannot keep people within one religious denomination unless they are united by common, visible signs or sacraments. Sacraments are needed for salvation because our God-given human nature requires that our minds be led to spiritual things by bodily and material things. We form concepts from percepts. This is in part because we are diseased in sin by inappropriate love for bodily things and pleasures, and it is appropriate that God provides a spiritual medicine that also works through the senses. The sacraments provide the right bodily exercises—ones that draw us away from improper worship and harmful, sinful actions. It is of the greatest importance to note, in response to objectors, that Christ's Passion is indeed the sufficient cause of our salvation, but *the sacraments obtain their power through his Passion.* "Christ's Passion is, so to say, applied to man through the sacraments."[320]

What effects do sacraments have on us?

First, the sacraments provide us with God's *grace,* and grace is an awesome thing! Thomas writes, "Grace is nothing else than a participated likeness of the Divine Nature, according to 2 Pet. 1:4: *He hath given us most great and precious promises; that we may be* [Vulgate—*you may be made*] *partakers of the Divine Nature.*"[321] Sacraments do not merely point to higher, spiritual things. They are "both causes and signs," which is to say, "They effect what they signify."[322] Sacraments, we might say, don't just

---

[320] Ibid. Thomas also cites Romans 5:3 "All we who are baptized in Christ Jesus, are baptized in His death."
[321] *ST*, III, Q. 62, art. 1.
[322] Ibid.

Sacrament	Virtues	The Sacred Seven, Parallels to the Bodily and Social Perfections of Humans
Baptism	Faith	Birth
Confirmation	Fortitude	Growth
Eucharist	Charity	Nourishment
Penance**	Justice	ɩ ealing sickness
Anointing of the Sick***	Hope	Restoration of health and vigor
Holy Orders	Prudence	Ruling and public acts
Matrimony	Temperance	Propagation of the species

* Culled from *ST*, III, Q. 65, art. 1.
** Also known as Reconciliation or Confession.
*** Called Extreme Unction in the *Summa Theologica*.

talk about it; they "get the job done." And as we will see in just a minute, the "jobs" the sacraments do serve to perfect us spiritually in a variety of ways. They are remedies to all kinds of sin and help perfect all kinds of virtues.

Secondly, some sacraments (Baptism, Confirmation, and Holy Orders) produce in our souls an enduring, indelible "character," "mark," or "seal." Thomas notes, "The Apostle says (2

Side-by-Side*

Counters to Defects and Penalties Resulting from Sin	Defects of sin
Original sin	Absence of spiritual life
Spiritual weakness	Infirmity of soul
Malice	The soul's tendency to sin
Mortal sin	Actual sin after Baptism
Venial sin	The remainder of sins not removed by Penance (either through negligence or ignorance when making a confession)
Ignorance	Divisions in the community
Concupiscence	Concupiscence in the individual and against decrease in a population

Cor. 1:21–22): *He . . . that hath anointed us is God: Who also hath sealed us, and given the pledge of the spirit in our hearts.* But a character means nothing else than a kind of sealing. Therefore it seems that by the sacraments, God imprints His character on us."[323] As ancient enlisted soldiers would receive bodily

[323] *ST*, III, Q. 63, art. 1.

markings to identify whom they served, God provides a spiritual seal on the souls of those who serve him. The eternal Character is Christ himself (Heb. 1:3). This is the character we share through the sacraments. A character provides us with permanent spiritual power. Baptism gives one the power to receive other sacraments; Confirmation strengthens that power; and Holy Orders conveys the power to provide sacraments to others by participating in Christ's priesthood. These characters can never be blotted from the soul, which is why these three sacraments are received only *once* in a person's life.

How do the seven sacraments relate to virtues and sins?

"The Church is said to be built up with the sacraments *which flowed from the side of Christ while hanging on the Cross.*"[324] Building upon the revelation of the Scriptures, Christ's Church administers seven sacraments. In the chapters ahead we'll spend several minutes on St. Thomas's examinations of each and every one of them, in how they fight sin, bolster virtue, and draw us closer to God. For now, as a thought-appetizer, I'll just lay this summary on the table.

[324] *ST*, III, Q. 64, art. 3.

CHAPTER THIRTY-FOUR

Baptism: The Gateway to Heaven

---

*Our Lord said (Matt. 28:19): Going . . . teach
ye all nations, baptizing them in the name of the
Father, and of the Son, and of the Holy Ghost.*
—ST, III, Q. 66, art. 5

Baptism has been called "the door of the sacraments," because
"it confers on man the power to receive other sacraments of the
Church."[325] Baptism washes away Original Sin and other past
sins and enrolls us as members of the Body of Christ, producing in us an indelible mark or character through the power of
Christ's Passion and Resurrection. The visible sign of the water
represents the cleansing of sin, and also our rebirth in Christ.

"Our Lord said (John 3:5); Unless a man be born again of
water and the Holy Ghost, he cannot enter into the kingdom
of God."[326] Baptism provides the grace that joins us in the Body
of Christ. We are the parts of the Body, and Christ is the Head.
As the head directs the body's movements, so do we receive
knowledge and truth from Christ, which provide spiritual guidance for our actions.

[325] *ST*, III, Q. 63, art. 6.
[326] *ST*, III, Q. 60, art. 5.

This effect of Baptism is called enlightenment. Another effect of Baptism is called fruitfulness. Psalm 22:2 says, "He hath brought me up on the water of refreshment; a gloss says that the sinner's soul, sterilized by drought, is made fruitful by Baptism."[327] The good fruits brought forth by Baptism are the good works we do as Christians. Baptism prepares us to receive the other graces proffered by the other sacraments, and its ultimate effect is to open the gates of heaven to us by removing the debt of guilt and punishment of sin that would otherwise block our entry.

How does the Church administer Baptism?

While immersing or sprinkling the recipient with water, the Church heeds Christ's explicit instructions: "The Latins baptize under this form: I baptize thee in the name of the Father, and of the Son, and of the Holy Ghost; whereas the Greeks use the following form: The servant of God, N. . . . is baptized in the name of the Father, etc."[328] Since the Church teaches that Baptism is necessary for salvation, it is very important to understand just what this means. Ideally, a Baptism is performed by a priest in the context of an entire liturgical rite, complete with the renunciation of Satan by the recipient or by the parent and godparent, with prayers and an anointing with a sacred chrism.[329] But not all these things are necessary.

[327] ST, III, Q. 69, art. 6.
[328] ST, III, Q. 60, art. 8. The "etc." means they also explicitly name the Son and the Holy Spirit too. That this remains the case in the Latin and Eastern liturgies today can be seen in the Catechism of the Catholic Church, no. 1240.
[329] A fragrant mixture of olive and balsam oils blessed by a bishop.

Because of the indelible character of a valid Baptism using water, done in the name of the Father, Son, and Holy Spirit, Thomas reported that the Church would consider valid such Baptisms performed by people who were not priests—by laymen, by heretics, indeed, even by "pagans," or non-Christians. Such Baptisms should occur only in emergencies. He even provides an extreme example of two pagans facing death who desired to be baptized—wherein one could baptize the other, who in turn would baptize him.[330] As for those who never get to receive the water and words of the sacrament of Baptism, the Church duly recognizes the "baptism of desire." A person desiring Baptism who dies before receiving it "can obtain salvation without being actually baptized, on account of his desire for Baptism, which desire is the outcome of faith that worketh by charity, whereby God, Whose power is not tied to visible sacraments, sanctifies man inwardly."[331]

---

[330] *ST*, III, Q. 67, art. 6.
[331] *ST*, III, Q. 68, art. 2.

CHAPTER THIRTY-FIVE

Confirmation: Onward, Christian Soldier!

---

*The sacraments of the New Law are ordained
unto special effects of grace; and therefore where
there is a special effect of grace, there we
find a special sacrament for the purpose.*

—*ST*, III, Q. 71, art. 1

Christ confirmed no one — how can the Church call Confirmation a sacrament?

Good question (sort of). We should recall that Christ did not baptize anyone either, but he mostly clearly gave his Church the mission to go forth and baptize to the ends of the earth. As for Christ's institution of Confirmation, Thomas opines, "We must say that Christ instituted this sacrament not by bestowing, but by promising it, according to John 16:7; *If I go not, the Paraclete will not come to you, but if I go, I will send Him to you.* And this was because in this sacrament the fullness of the Holy Ghost is bestowed, which was not to be given before Christ's Resurrection and Ascension; according to John 7:39: *As yet the Spirit was not given, because Jesus was not yet glorified.*"[332]

---

[332] *ST*, III, Q. 72, art. 1.

We have seen that the grace of Baptism produces a spiritual birth. Spiritual growth can be seen to parallel bodily growth in man. The child moves toward the perfection of his powers as he approaches adulthood with the ability to act as an adult—"hence the Apostle says (1 Cor. 13:11): When I became a man, I put away the things of a child." Through the grace of Confirmation we are strengthened in the maturity of our faith by a special outpouring of the Holy Spirit, which includes, as we saw in chapter 16, the Holy Spirit's gift of fortitude.

How and why does the Church administer Confirmation?

As for the sensible signs of this sacrament, the Church uses chrism, a perfumed oil. This practice has deep scriptural roots. "Now the grace of the Holy Ghost is signified by oil; hence Christ is said to be anointed with the oil of gladness (Ps. 44:8), by reason of His being gifted with the fullness of the Holy Ghost."[333] As for the balm that is added to perfume the oil, "the Apostle says (2 Cor. 2:15), We are the good odor of Christ."[334] Further, it is written (Ecclus. 24:21): My odor is as the purest balm."[335]

As for the minister of this sacrament, it is the bishop who lays hands on the recipient of the sacrament, anoints with chrism, and pronounces the words of the rite of Confirmation, invoking the spiritual seal of the Holy Spirit.

Why the bishop for Confirmation, while priests administer Baptism? "Though he who is baptized is made a member of the

---

[333] *ST*, III, Q. 72, art. 1 (Psalm 45:7 in the RSV).
[334] Ibid.
[335] Ibid. (In the RSV, this appears to be Sir. 24:15: "like choice myrhh I spread a pleasant odor.")

Church, nevertheless he is not yet enrolled as a Christian soldier. And therefore he is brought to the bishop, as to the commander of the army."[336]

As for becoming a "Christian soldier," this surely seems to be an idea whose time has come again today. In our increasingly secular world, as the rights of Christians are increasingly attacked and encroached upon in ways they have not been since the early centuries of the primitive Church, we need to embrace this idea, to "put on the whole armor of God" (Eph. 6:10) and prepare to "fight the good fight of faith" (1 Tim. 6:12) in ways we may not have imagined just a few years ago. We'll need to develop the virtue of fortitude and to grow in the grace of the Holy Spirit's gift of fortitude that strengthened our souls when we were confirmed. With St. Thomas as our guide, onward Christian soldiers!

[336] *ST*, III, Q. 71, art. 10.

CHAPTER THIRTY-SIX

The Holy Eucharist: The "Hidden Deity"

Devoutly I adore You, hidden Deity
Under these appearances concealed.
To you my heart surrenders self
For, seeing You, all else must yield.

—St. Thomas Aquinas, "Devoutly
I Adore You, Hidden Deity"[337]

Within the *Summa Theologica*, Aquinas is ever the philosopher and theologian, treating the most wondrous mysteries of the faith with careful and subtle logical arguments, expounding and defending them while testing the very limits of frail human reason. We must never lose sight of the fact, however, that even more than a learned Doctor of the Church, St. Thomas was a saintly man who loved God above all else. That he experienced God *in his head* like few before him or since rings out from every page of the *Summa*. That he experienced God even more deeply *in his heart* might not be as apparent to some.

---

[337] This is the first stanza of St. Thomas's prayer *Adoro Te Devote, Latens Deitas*, as it appears in Anderson and Moser, *The Aquinas Prayer Book*, 69.

That is why, before we take a minute to examine of few of Thomas's profound thoughts on the sacrament of the Eucharist, I wanted to direct readers to the beautiful and moving prayers and hymns St. Thomas wrote on many of the doctrines he argued in a scholarly way in the *Summa*. They are true stirrings of his soul, revealing how much he loved and worshipped him whom he sought to understand more deeply.

Next, we'll move to Thomas's deep reflections on that "hidden deity," to see just why, as he wrote, "the sacrament of the Eucharist is the greatest of all the sacraments."[338]

What are three reasons the Eucharist is the greatest of all sacraments?

While other sacraments are in various ways instruments through which we share in Christ's power, the sacrament of the Eucharist contains Christ himself.

All the other sacraments point to the Eucharist is some way as their end.[339] Baptism prepares one to receive the Eucharist. Confirmation perfects one so as not to fear to defend the Eucharist. Penance and Anointing of the Sick prepare one to receive worthily the Body of Christ. Holy Orders bestow on the priest the power of consecration of the Eucharist. Even Matrimony signifies in a way the union of Christ with the Church, "hence the Apostle says," when referring to matrimony (Eph. 5:32): This is a great sacrament; but I speak in Christ and in the Church."[340]

---

[338] *ST*, III, Q. 65, art. 3.
[339] The *Catechism of the Catholic Church* notes the Eucharist as "the source and summit of the Christian life" (no. 1324).
[340] *ST*, III, Q. 65, art. 3.

Nearly all the liturgical rites of the sacraments culminate in the Eucharist itself, as when those who are ordained receive Holy Communion and when those being baptized as adults receive their first Holy Communion at the same Mass.

How is the Eucharist of the past, the present, and the future?

We see this through its various names. In relation to the past, it is called a *Sacrifice*, since it commemorates Christ's Passion. In relation to the present, it is called *Communion* because it unifies the Church. As St. John Damascene wrote, "It is called Communion because we communicate with Christ through it, both because we partake of his flesh and Godhead, and because we communicate with and are united to one another through it."[341] In relation to the future, when the Anointing of the Sick is administered, Holy Communion is referred to as *Viaticum*—literally "food for the journey"—because Christ himself feeds and perfects the soul on its way to everlasting life.

What is transubstantiation?

Transubstantiation is the term the Church uses to describe the mysterious conversion of the bread and wine into the Body and Blood of Christ himself at the Consecration of the sacrament of the Eucharist. Christ Himself, of course, initiated the sacrament of the Eucharist and the Catholic Church literally takes the Word at his word when he says that "my flesh is meat indeed: and my blood is drink indeed" (John 6:56 [RSV: 6:55]). This was a "hard saying" (John 6:61 [RSV: 6:60]) to hear, even among his disciples, but the Church has believed it and sought

[341] ST, III, Q. 73, art. 4.

to understand it better—from the moment Christ initiated the Eucharist before his Passion, per the descriptions in the Gospels of Matthew, Mark, and Luke.

Even so, transubstantiation (*trans* = change, *substantiation* derives from substance) is hard to wrap our minds around. We acquire knowledge through our senses. The sensible *accidents*—the material appearances of bread and wine—remain while their *substance* (what they really are) becomes the Body and Blood of Christ. (Hence St. Thomas's "hidden deity.") We "see" the deity through the "eyes" of faith, trusting in the words of Christ himself.

To make things a little bit clearer, Thomas notes that any change in nature is a change in a thing's form in various ways, not in its very substance. Water, for example, in a natural change, may turn into ice or steam, but it does not change into blood. Transubstantiation is a *supernatural* change. God, and only God, as "infinite Act" and the cause of all being, can change things in their very being, not just in their form, but in the substance of what they are. Indeed, "the author of being can change into whatever there is of being in the other, withdrawing that whereby it was distinguished from the other."[342] How odd that some Christians who grant that God created all that we see out of nothing, would not grant him the power to be truly present in the sacrament of the Eucharist.

[342] *ST*, III, Q. 75, art. 4.

DUMB OX BOX #10
Should we pray to the saints in heaven or to God alone?

In St. Thomas's day, there were those who said: "It would seem that we ought to pray to God alone. Prayer is an act of religion . . . But God alone is to be worshipped by religion. Therefore we should pray to God alone." (All quotations in this section are from *ST*, II-II, Q. 83, art. 4). Note that this is an objection that Thomas goes on to dispel.

Thomas notes that prayer is offered to a person in two ways: "first, as to be filled by him, secondly, as to be obtained through him." We pray in the first way to God alone, for only he has the power to supply the grace and glory we request from him. We pray to the saints, whether they be human or angelic, in the second way only, but not because God does not know our petitions unless they tell him. It is so that our prayers may be made more effective through the saints' prayers and merits. We see this clearly in Apocalypse 8:4, where it notes, "*the smoke of the incense,* namely *the prayers of the saints, ascended up before God.*"

St. Thomas Aquinas, "Pray for us!"

CHAPTER THIRTY-SEVEN

Penance: The Escape from Sin

On the contrary, Our Lord said (Luke 13:3); Unless you shall do penance, you shall all likewise perish.

—*ST*, III, Q. 84, art. 5

Is the sacrament of Penance necessary for salvation?

St. Thomas says, "A thing is necessary for salvation in two ways; first, absolutely; secondly on a supposition. A thing is absolutely necessary for salvation, if no one can obtain salvation without it—for example, the grace of Christ, and the sacrament of Baptism, whereby a man is born again in Christ. The sacrament of Penance is necessary on a supposition, for it is necessary, not for all, but for those who are in sin."[343]

Where is the sacrament of Penance in the Bible?

The words uttered by the priest in the sacrament of Penance: "I absolve thee in the name of the Father, and of the Son, and

---

[343] *ST*, III, Q. 84, art. 5.

of the Holy Ghost"[344] are based upon the words Christ spoke to Peter when he said: "Whatsoever thou shalt loose upon earth, it shall be loosed also in heaven" (Matt. 16:19) and from the words he spoke to his disciples when he said: "Whose sins you shall forgive, they are forgiven them; and whose sins you shall retain, they are retained" (John 20:23). Therefore, the priest does not pray that God have mercy or will grant the penitent absolution, but *he declares the deed done*. It is God who actually absolves and forgives sins, but he does so through the priests to whom he has delegated the authority to serve as the instrument of his divine power. Thomas notes, "It would be a more complete explanation to say that the words, *I absolve thee* mean: *I grant thee the sacrament of absolution*.[345]

When is a sacrament a virtue as well?

St. Thomas writes that there is a sense in which penance is itself a virtue related to justice, complete with integral parts. Further, the sacrament of Penance works through God's grace to restore other virtues deadened by sin. The integral parts of the virtue of penance that Thomas explains in question 85 of Part III of the *Summa Theologica* are the same three parts you will find in paragraphs 1451 through 1460 in the *Catechism of the Catholic Church* on the sacrament of Reconciliation — namely, *contrition*, *confession of sins*, and *satisfaction*. When we are truly penitent, we appeal to God's justice and mercy by feeling sorrow within our hearts for our sins (*contrition*), by outwardly admitting them to the priest (*confession*), and by "doing penance," that is, by making amends by the actions prescribed by the

[344] *ST*, III, Q. 84, art. 3.
[345] *ST*, III, Q. 84, art. 4.

priest (*satisfaction*), be they prayers, reflections, good deeds, or specific acts of reparation. And penance is a virtue (and sacrament) to be practiced again and again. When Thomas considered how often it could be repeated, he recalled Christ's words about how often we should forgive our brother: "*Seventy times seven times.*"[346]

When did words turn to straw?

As Thomas worked on the treatise on Penance in the *Summa Theologica*, he had his famous mystical experience of Christ, after which he announced he could write no more. What he had written seemed "like straw" after what he had seen, perhaps having been given a glimpse of the beatific vision. Not long after, on March 7, 1274, Thomas, not yet fifty years old, joined Christ in heaven. Thankfully for us, his friend Brother Reginald of Piperno completed Thomas's work, borrowing from Thomas's older writings on the *Sentences* of Peter Lombard. Next we'll take just a couple of minutes to look at the "Supplement" to the *Summa's* Part III.

[346] *ST*, III, Q. 84, art. 10; citing from Matt. 23:21 and implying no limit.

CHAPTER THIRTY-EIGHT

Last Rites: To Prepare the Soul for Rising

Now Extreme Unction is a spiritual remedy,
since it avails for the remission of sins, according
to James 5:15. Therefore it is a sacrament.

—*ST*, Supp., Q. 29, art. 1

Extreme Unction, what's your function?

In St. Thomas's time the sacrament we call today the Anointing of the Sick was called Extreme Unction: *unction* for the use of an *unguent*, or oil for anointing, and *extreme* for those who were *in extremis*, or near death. The sacrament involves anointing the sick with consecrated oil for the remission of sins, and we see it prescribed in James 5:14–15: "Is any man sick among you? Let him bring in the priests of the church, and let them pray over him, anointing him with oil in the name of the Lord. And the prayer of faith shall save the sick man: and the Lord shall raise him up: and if he be in sins, they shall be forgiven him."

Thomas notes as well, that although the Gospels do not mention Christ *administering* this sacrament, the Lord did and said many things that were not written down. (Recall that last verse in St. John's Gospel.) Further, "as a matter of fact, however, an anointing done by the apostles is mentioned in the Gospel (Mark 6:13) where it is said that they anointed the sick with oil."[347] In this way, then, the institution of the sacrament was made known by the actions of the apostles. Christ did not *receive* this sacrament, for the same reason he did not receive the sacrament of Penance, because he committed no sins.

This sacrament produces *spiritual* healing by divine power, but *bodily* healing does not always follow, unless it is required for the spiritual healing in accordance with God's will.

[347] ST, Supp., Q. 29, art. 3.

CHAPTER THIRTY-NINE

Holy Orders:
Granting "Spiritual Power"

I answer that, *The Master's definition of Order*
applies to Order as a sacrament of the Church.
Hence he mentions two things, namely, the outward
sign, a kind of seal, i.e., a kind of sign, and the
inward effect, whereby spiritual power, etc."[348]

—*ST*, Supp., Q. 34, art. 2

Where did Holy Orders come from, and what do they do?

Thomas recognized "Order" as one of the seven sacraments of the Church. Indeed, in a sense: "Now, Order is the cause of man being the dispenser of the other sacraments. Therefore Order has more reason for being a sacrament than the others."[349] The ordained individual receives an indelible seal on his soul, as is the case with those baptized and confirmed.

[348] "The Master" in the quotation above refers to Peter Lombard. You'll recall that the Supplement to the *Summa Theologica* that Reginald of Piperno put together was culled largely from St. Thomas's writings on Lombard's *Sentences*, the standard masterwork of theology in his day.

[349] *ST*, Supp., Q. 34, art. 3.

Order was established first by Christ himself: "The apos-tles received the power of Order before the Ascension (John 20:22), where it is said: *Receive the Holy Ghost.*"[350] Indeed, the next verse is one we discussed in the chapter on Penance, whereby Christ gave the apostle authority to administer that sacrament: "Whose sins you shall forgive, they are forgiven them; and whose sins you shall retain, they are retained" (John 20:23). Priests receive the chalice and paten at ordination in recognition of the power they receive to consecrate the Body and Blood of Christ in the greatest of all the sacraments. The Church Fathers described Holy Orders as a remedy to ignorance, although we must note that "it does not mean that by receiving Orders a man has his ignorance driven out of him, but that the recipient of Orders is set in authority to expel ignorance among the people."[351] The *primary teaching authority belongs to bishops and ultimately to the Pope.*

[350] *ST*, Supp., Q. 35, art. 4.
[351] Ibid., art. 1.

DUMB OX BOX #11

I get distracted when I pray. Does God stop listening?

No, He doesn't. One of St. Thomas's own questions is "Whether Attention Is a Necessary Condition of Prayer" His answer may be a bit of a surprise (and perhaps a relief): "Purposely to allow one's mind to wander in prayer is sinful, and hinders the prayer from having fruit . . . But to wander in mind unintentionally does not deprive the prayer of fruit" (*ST*, II-II, Q. 83, art. 13).

Thomas lists three main *effects* of prayer: 1) *merit*, which comes from all acts inspired by the love of God, 2) *impetration*, the production of petitions or requests to God, and 3) the *spiritual refreshment* of the mind of the one who prays. For the first two effects, simply the initial intention to pray is sufficient, even if attention is lost, although one must have the initial intention. For the last, the immediate effect of spiritual refreshment of the mind comes only while paying attention.

Further, Thomas describes three *kinds of attention* we can bring to vocal prayer: 1) attention *to the words* so we say them right, 2) attention to the *meaning* of the words, and 3) attention to the *end* or goal of the prayer—that is, God. Here, *only the third is essential.* Thomas notes that even the slow-witted who can't remember or understand the words of certain prayers are still able, within their limits, to raise their thoughts to God. Further, even among the learned and holy, *"this attention, whereby the mind is fixed on God, is sometimes so strong that the mind forgets all other things"* (ST, II-II, Q. 83, art. 13).

So, to put it in a Thomistic nutshell, no one is more aware than God of the limitations of our human nature, fleeting attention and all. God appreciates the fact that we try to pray, even when our wandering minds go astray!

CHAPTER FORTY

Matrimony: Conferring Grace upon Nature

*Hence others say that matrimony, inasmuch
as it is contracted in the faith of Christ, is able to
confer the grace which enables us to do those works
which are required in matrimony; and this is more
probable, since wherever God gives the faculty to
do a thing, He gives also the help whereby man
is enabled to make becoming use of that faculty.*

—*ST*, Supp., Q. 42, art. 3

Is Matrimony natural, and is it sacramental?

Thomas's, Peter Lombard's, and the Catholic Church's recognition of the importance of marriage between a man and a woman can be seen in the details of the 26 questions and 110 pages they receive in the Supplement to the *Summa Theologica*. We have here but a minute to highlight a couple of points. First, marriage falls under *natural law*. Citing the authority of Aristotle, who rightly called man a *rational animal* and a *political animal*, Thomas writes: "The Philosopher (Ethic. viii, 12) says that *man is animal more inclined by nature to connubial than political society*. But *man is naturally a political and gregarious animal*, as the same author asserts (Polit. i, 2). Therefore, he is naturally inclined to connubial union, thus the conjugal union or matrimony is natural."[352] We are naturally inclined to join to beget children; hence Aristotle notes the three main things we get from our parents are *existence, nourishment,* and *education.* Parents must stay together so that the latter can be best provided.

As for the sacramental nature of Matrimony, "Holy Writ states there has been matrimony from the beginning of the human race," and as we read in Matthew 25:6: "What . . . God hath joined together let no man put asunder." [353]

[352] *ST,* Supp., Q. 41, art. 1. *Connubial* indicates the relationship between man and wife.
[353] Ibid.

CHAPTER FORTY-ONE

The Body's Resurrection — to Perfection

Man will rise again at the most perfect state of nature. Now human nature, because as God founded human nature without a defect, even so will He restore it without defect.

—ST, Supp., Q. 81, art. 1

What will our glorified bodies be like?

"It is written (Eph. 4:13): *Until we all meet . . . unto a perfect man, unto the measure of the age of the fullness of Christ.*"[354] After the Resurrection, we will be united with our *material* bodies, but God will perfect them *spiritually*. Thomas speculates that we will rise again in a youthful state, in our thirties, as did Jesus Christ, and our bodies will possess four spiritual perfections throughout eternal life. Those qualities are as follows:

> **Impassibility:** The glorified body will not suffer pain, disease, corruption, or death as, "according to 1 Cor. 15:42, It is sown in corruption, it shall rise in incorruption."[355]

[354] *ST*, Supp., Q. 81, art. 1.
[355] *ST*, Supp., Q. 82, art. 1.

Subtlety: The glorified body will be able to penetrate or pass through material objects as Christ did in his glorified body. "It is written (1 Cor. 15:44): *It is sown a corruptible body, it shall rise a spiritual, i.e., a spirit-like, body.*"[356] The actions of the glorified body will be completely subject to the spirit.

Agility: The glorified body will move effortlessly at great speeds and distances. "It is written (Isa. 40:31): *They shall run and not be weary, they shall walk and not faint.*"[357]

Clarity: The glorified body will be beautiful and radiant: "It is written (Matt. 13:43): *The just shall shine as the sun in the kingdom of their father.*"[358]

---

[356] *ST*, Supp., Q. 83, art. 1.
[357] Ibid., art. 2.
[358] *ST*, Supp., Q. 85, art. 1.

CHAPTER FORTY-TWO

Last Things Last

> *The desire of the saints to know all things*
> *will be fulfilled by the mere fact of their seeing*
> *God; just as their desire to possess all good*
> *things will be fulfilled by their possessing God.*
>
> —*ST*, Supp., Q. 92, art. 3

What joy will fulfill us and last forever?

The word *last* in the chapter title has several different meanings. We come now to the *last* topic we'll address in the *Summa Theologica*. It deals with the greatest of the "four *last* things": death, judgment, heaven, and hell. It is our *last* or final end as creatures of God, and *last*, but not least, it will *last* eternally.

Thomas speaks here of the reason we were created and the reason for Christ's Incarnation so that we might enjoy the eternal bliss of the beatific vision—of that font and perfection of all that is good—of the essence of God himself. The vision of our bodily senses cannot see the essence of God, who is Spirit. We will not even be able to see him as he is with the eyes of our own glorified bodies.

"In the vision wherein God will be seen in His essence, the Divine Essence itself will be the form, as it were, of the intellect, by which it will understand: nor is it necessary for them to become one in being, but only to become one as regards to the act of understanding."[359] God will enable our glorified souls to see, know, and be present with him — and this will satisfy our souls. Although our eternal bliss will be chiefly of the soul, it will "overflow" into the body as well.

"Yet our body will have a certain beatitude from seeing God in sensible creatures; and especially in Christ's body."[360] Christ said he would manifest himself to the saints in heaven (John 19:21). What a glorious sight that will be!

[359] ST, Supp., Q. 92, art. 1.
[360] Ibid., art. 3.

DUMB OX BOX #12
Why was our Lord's Cross a cross?

"Not without purpose did he choose this class of death, that He might be a teacher of that breadth and height, and length, and depth, of which the Apostle speaks (Eph. 3:18)" (ST, III, Q. 46, art. 4). Thomas borrows this beautiful metaphorical lesson on the dimensions of Christ's Cross from the writings of St. Augustine of Hippo.

Breadth: The breadth of the crossbeam represents *good works*, since Christ's hands were spread out upon it.

Length: The length of the Cross from the crossbeam to the ground, where it is planted, stands, and abides, represents the virtue of *longanimity*, which bears all things over time.

Height: The height of the Cross from the crossbeam to its top held the head of the crucified Christ, who is the *supreme desire and hope* of believers.

Depth: The depth of the Cross, hidden in the earth from view, that holds it fixed is like the root from which the entire tree grows, and this represents the depth of God's *gratuitous grace*.

Indeed, said Augustine: *"The tree upon which were fixed the members of Him dying was even the chair of the Master teaching"* (ST, III, Q. 45, art. 4).

Think on all this the next time you see a crucifix!

The One-Lifetime Aquinas

He [Thomas Aquinas] enlightened the Church more than all the other Doctors together; a man can derive more profit from his books in one year than from a lifetime spent pondering the philosophy of others.

—Pope Pius X, citing
Pope John XXII, *Doctoris Angelici*

Can you name three lessons from St. Thomas in one minute?

Wonder: St. Thomas approached every part of creation with awe, since each part reflects, in some small way, the perfection of God. This wonder prompted the continual, deep, study and contemplation that Thomas passed on to us in wonderful books. May they fire such wonder in us.

Gratitude: As Thomas looked with wonder at the truth, beauty, and goodness of Creation, he never lost sight of the fact that it all came to be and is sustained as a purely gratuitous gift of God. May we show gratitude to Thomas for showing both *why* and *how* we should perpetually show our gratitude toward God.

Love: The fires of charity burned with a solar intensity within the soul of the Angelic Doctor. Although earthly kings sought him out and princes of the Church sought to grant him great titles, St. Thomas loved nothing more than to contemplate and share the truth as a humble Dominican friar. His exhausting studies, teaching, writing, and priestly duties may have led to his early earthly demise. We might well say that he laid down his life for us, his friends. Above all, we learn from him and his works how we can better love ourselves, our neighbor, and God, with all our heart, mind, and strength.

Kevin Vost

Kevin Vost (b. 1961) holds a Doctor of Psychology in Clinical Psychology (Psy.D.) degree from the Adler School of Professional Psychology in Chicago. He has taught at Aquinas College in Nashville, the University of Illinois at Springfield, MacMurray College, and Lincoln Land Community College. He has served as a research review committee member for American Mensa, a society promoting the scientific study of human intelligence, and as an advisory board member for the International Association of Resistance Trainers, an organization that certifies personal fitness trainers. Dr. Vost drinks great drafts of coffee while studying timeless, Thomistic tomes in the company of his wife, two sons, and their puppy, in Springfield, Illinois.

An Invitation

Reader, the book that you hold in your hands was published by Sophia Institute Press. Sophia Institute seeks to nurture the spiritual, moral, and cultural life of souls and to spread the Gospel of Christ in conformity with the authentic teachings of the Roman Catholic Church.

Our press fulfills this mission by offering translations, reprints, and new publications that afford readers a rich source of the enduring wisdom of mankind.

We also operate two popular online Catholic resources: CrisisMagazine.com and CatholicExchange.com.

Crisis Magazine provides insightful cultural analysis that arms readers with the arguments necessary for navigating the ideological and theological minefields of the day. *Catholic Exchange* provides world news from a Catholic perspective as well as daily devotionals and articles that will help you to grow in holiness and live a life consistent with the teachings of the Church.

Sophia Institute Press also serves as the publisher for the Thomas More College of Liberal Arts and Holy Spirit College. Both colleges provide university-level education under the guiding light of Catholic teaching. If you know a young person seeking a college that takes seriously the adventure of learning and the quest for truth, please bring these institutions to his attention.

www.SophiaInstitute.com
www.CatholicExchange.com
www.CrisisMagazine.com